This book is dedicated to the many volunteers who freely give their knowledge, skills and time to the cause of protecting and sharing our aerospace heritage.

Aircraft of the Aerospace Museum of California

McClellan, California 95652

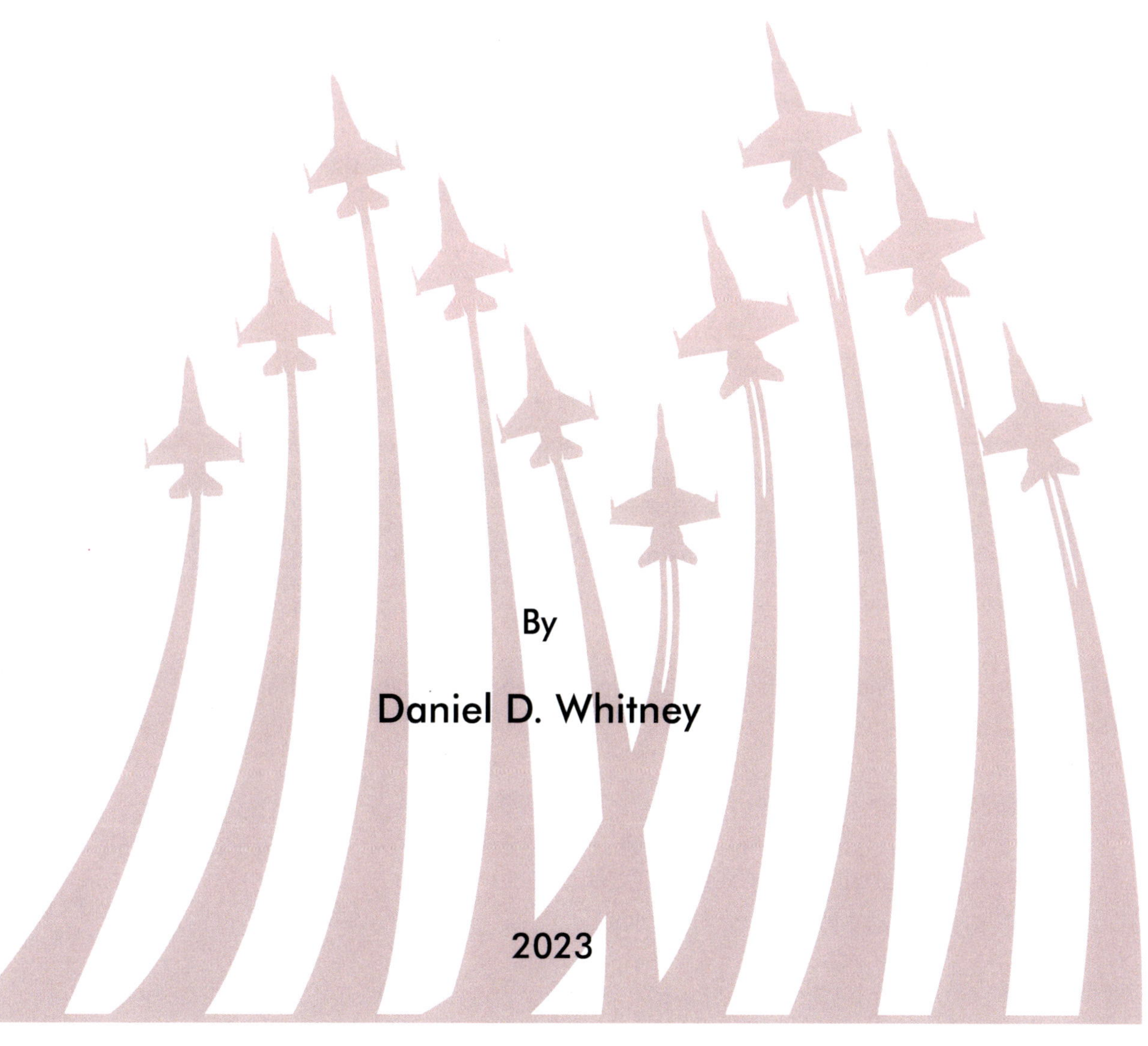

By

Daniel D. Whitney

2023

About the Author

Daniel D. Whitney is a retired engineer living in the Sacramento area and a long-time volunteer with the Aerospace Museum of California. As such he has served the Museum Foundation as both a Board Member and its President.

His civilian career was as a nuclear and mechanical engineer in the electrical utility industry. Aviation has always been near to his heart, harkening to when he served in the USAF as an Aircraft Maintenance Officer on C-130E aircraft during the Vietnam War. He currently serves on the museum Curatorial Committee, where his lifelong interest in aircraft engines is focused on supporting the museum's world-class engine collection. His prior book is *Vee's For Victory! The Story of the Allison V-1710.*

ISBN: 9798375101750

Book designed by Daniel D. Whitney

All photographs by Daniel D. Whitney, or as noted, by Elizabeth Payne

Forth Edition, March 2023

Published by Aerospace Museum of California
3200 Freedom Park Drive, McClellan, CA 95652

To purchase additional copies of this book, please contact the Aerospace Museum of California www.aerospacemuseumofcalifornia.org

Printed in the United States of America

Table of Contents

Welcome to the *Aerospace Museum of California*, located at McClellan Park, near Sacramento, California.

This book provides a visual tour of our extensive collection of historic aircraft, showing a progression of mankind's evolution from kites to balloons to bi-planes and on to supersonic jets, rockets, and spaceships. The Sacramento region has enjoyed a long and dynamic involvement with aviation and aerospace, stretching back to the time of the first powered flight in the early 20th Century. Local contemporaries of the Wright brothers were actively building airplanes at the time, which established a strong aviation community here in the years prior to the First World War. All this local aviation activity resulted in the manufacture of airplanes in Sacramento during that war. Mather Field was established in 1918 and became a major aviation and military presence that continues to this day. McClellan Field was added just prior to the Second World War and continued until 2001 as a major aerospace maintenance depot supporting U.S. interests in the Pacific and Far East. Our region's extensive focus on aviation and aerospace evolved rapidly between 1945 and 2010 as shown by the achievements of Aerojet Corporation, creators of advanced rockets for military, commercial space development, and deep space research and science missions.

The *Aerospace Museum of California* honors the past and inspires the future through STEAM (Science, Technology, Engineering, Art, and Math) education. Numerous studies have demonstrated outstanding synaptic and educational benefits for students who have the opportunity to learn and make firm connections across these pedagogical subject areas. The Aerospace Museum exists today because of a legacy of aerospace interest and support from the community, combined with a commitment to educate and inspire future generations of students and learners of all ages.

The story of how the museum came to be is important to the future of the museum. The museum's history, and it's standing in the Northern California community, affects the nature of the collection on display and the considerable support and contributions that enable the museum to meet its mission to educate and inspire students of all ages. In 2022, the museum's 40th anniversary year, our team inspired over 63,000 visitors including over 30,000 students. We actively honored the historic aviation and aerospace achievements of the past, while inspiring the future by providing STEAM educational opportunities to prepare students for important roles in our technologically complex world of today and the future.

The museum began as an outgrowth of the 1982 Air Force Heritage Program, whose original purpose was to promote knowledge of past accomplishments and pride in the U.S. Air Force. An underlying focus was to provide a training opportunity for development of young airmen and officers. The Air Force did not provide specific funding for these museums, however base commanders were authorized and encouraged to build museums from within their mission resources and priorities. McClellan was an ideal location for such a museum as it had access to many important aerospace artifacts and could benefit from utilizing the museum for supplemental training of staff and assigned personnel. With education as its foundation a not-for-profit 501(c)3 Museum Foundation was established in 1985 in three surplus buildings about a mile from the museum's current location. The public grand opening of the display center and initial collection of aircraft occurred in September 1986.

The museum's original aircraft displays and exhibits were the result of early training needs of the Air Force. Discarded, damaged or derelict aircraft were provided, challenging the skills of our early volunteers to provide viable exhibits. Several very rare airplanes were acquired and returned to display condition, while other aircraft were trucked in disassembled, and a further number flew their last flights to McClellan.

In 1995, the U.S. Air Force announced that McClellan Air Force Base would close in 2000, along with the museum. Both decisions were met with dismay, though the only one that could be challenged was the pending closure of the museum. The Air Force established criteria for communities desiring to keep their museums, and in 1998 the Museum Foundation volunteers, with considerable community support, met all requirements to transition the museum to civilian leadership. The 30 aircraft then on display would remain at McClellan on long-term loan from the *National Museum of the U.S. Air Force*.

As the base was in transition to become the McClellan Business Park it became necessary for the museum to relocate. The Museum Foundation was successful in purchasing six acres on the edge of the base, in Freedom Park, from the North Highlands Recreation and Park District. The move was completed in December 2003, followed by more fund raising and development that resulted in construction of the 37,500 square foot *Hardie Setzer Pavilion and Air Park*.

In its new facilities the museum has installed a highly utilized educational flight simulator laboratory where students are exposed to and trained in the skills and knowledge needed to proceed into flight training. Additional flight simulators are available to give visitors the flight experience, and numerous exhibits in the Pavilion cover diverse themes such as the history of flight, the role of Women in Aerospace, Air and Sea Rescue, Wind Energy Kites and an exhibit of the world's first Human-Powered Helicopter. Also featured is a world-class display of aircraft and rocket engines, key components in understanding the history and future of flight. These exhibits, augmented with dozens of STEAM education programs support the museum's mission and commitment to students and families. Tens of thousands of students participate in our education programs each year, along with hundreds who attend the museum's popular Summer Camps.

Staffing of the museum was originally accomplished by a dedicated corps of volunteers, which grew steadily from 50 to 60 in the 1980s-1990s to over 100 by 2010. In 2010, the administrative complexities of California business operations and facilities management required the museum to develop professional staffing to manage the daily functions, operations and fundraising required for a large and complex educational facility. Today the museum is managed by 12 full-time professional staff and educators, who partner with over 200 outstanding volunteers for technical knowledge, educational and operational support.

The *Aerospace Museum of California* is proud to be a Smithsonian Affiliate, which provides access to exhibits and artifacts that would otherwise be unavailable in Northern California. We are the *Smithsonian Air & Space Museum* in your neighborhood. We consistently grow our collection of artifacts and exhibits: today there are well over 40 aircraft in the collection with plans for more in the future. Restoration and maintenance of these historic aircraft is done by our dedicated volunteers, who demonstrate their pride in our history and aviation accomplishments by working to keep the collection inspiring, while minimizing the effects of time.

This revision of the book includes updates featuring eight aircraft that our volunteers have restored and put on display in the last several years. We hope this book will provide you with insight, details, and interesting stories about the aircraft and artifacts in our collection. We invite you to explore, discover and be inspired!

Thomas E. Jones
Executive Director
Aerospace Museum of California

ATTACK BOMBER-Korea/Vietnam

DOUGLAS A-1E *SKYRAIDER*

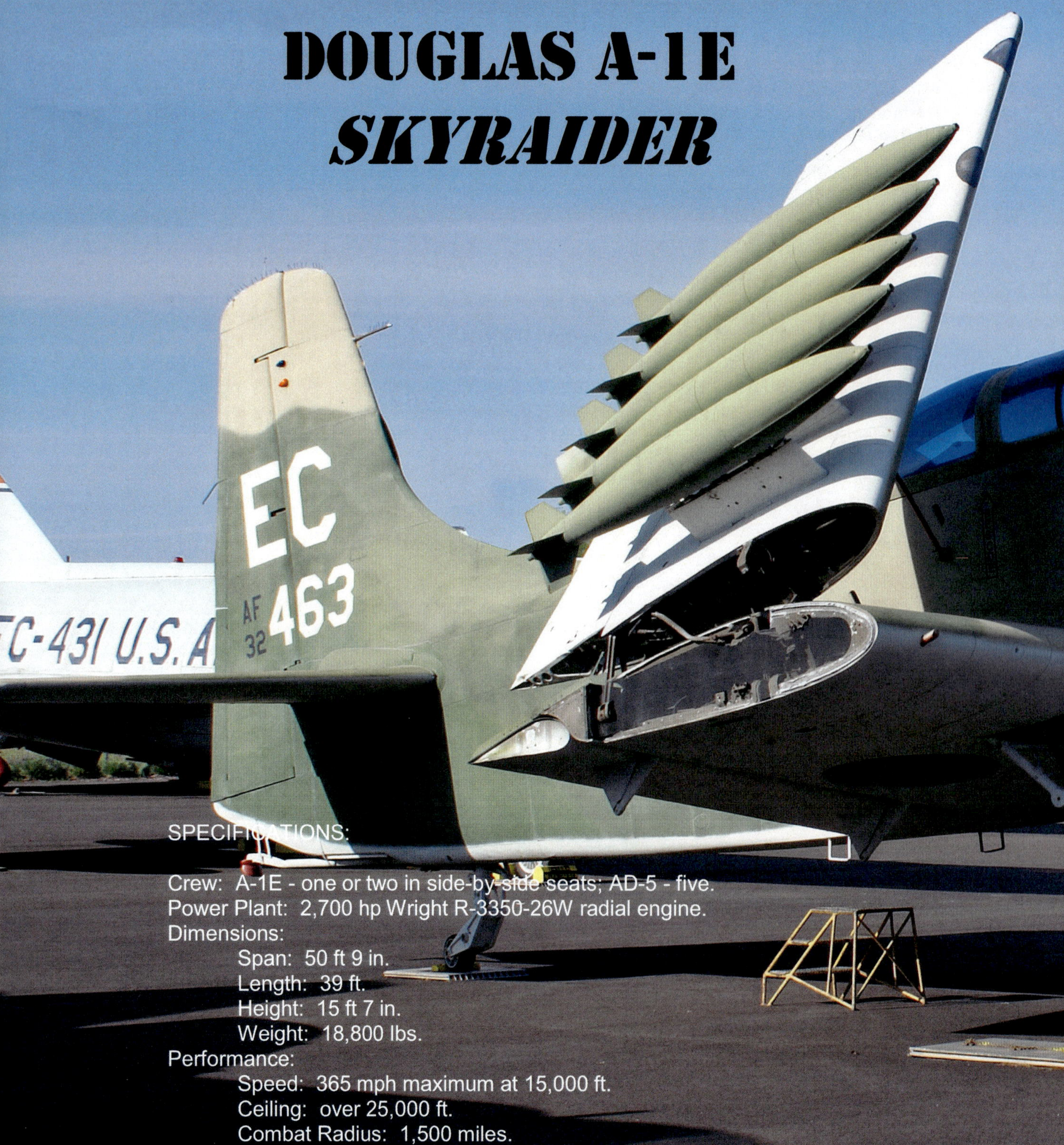

SPECIFICATIONS:

Crew: A-1E - one or two in side-by-side seats; AD-5 - five.
Power Plant: 2,700 hp Wright R-3350-26W radial engine.
Dimensions:
- Span: 50 ft 9 in.
- Length: 39 ft.
- Height: 15 ft 7 in.
- Weight: 18,800 lbs.

Performance:
- Speed: 365 mph maximum at 15,000 ft.
- Ceiling: over 25,000 ft.
- Combat Radius: 1,500 miles.

Armament: four 20 mm cannon, plus twelve wing stations for bombs and/or rockets.

THIS AIRCRAFT IS ON LOAN FROM THE NATIONAL MUSEUM OF THE USAF

Built by Douglas Aircraft Corp., the AD-5 (A-1E) entered service with the US Navy as an attack bomber prior to the Korean War. During the Vietnam War, 50 aircraft were taken from storage and used by USAF and RVN pilots for close support and rescue helicopter escort. Major Bernard Fisher flew one of these aircraft when he rescued a fellow pilot from behind enemy lines on March 10, 1966, becoming the first USAF Medal of Honor recipient during the Vietnam conflict.

U.S. Navy BuNo 132463 was one of 670 AD-5s built by Douglas at their El Segundo, California plant, and accepted by the Navy in February 1954. It served aboard the U.S.S. Shangri-la, U.S.S. Franklin Roosevelt, U.S.S. Intrepid, and U.S.S. Enterprise before being stricken from Navy records in July 1963. In 1962 AD-5s were redesignated as A-1Es. It was brought to the museum from storage in October 1985, and restored by the museum staff. It is painted in the markings of the 1st Special Operations Squadron, 14th Special Operations Wing.

MCDONNELL-DOUGLAS A-4C *SKYHAWK*

SPECIFICATIONS:
Crew: One
Powerplant: One Wright J65-W-20, 8,200 lbf thrust (36,475 newtons)
Dimensions :
- Wing span – 27 ft 6in (8.4 m)
- Length – 40 ft 4 in (12.3 m)
- Height – 15 ft 0 in. (4.6 m)
- Weight: Empty – 10,800 lbs (4,898 kg)
- Normal take-off - 24,500 lbs (11,111 kg)

Performance:
- Max speed with 4,000 lb bomb load – 561 mph, top speed – 646 mph (1,040 km/h)
- Range: 2,000 miles (3,220 km)

Armament:
Two 20 mm cannon in wing roots; provisions for several hundred variations of armament loads including bombs, missiles, ground attack pods, torpedoes, and countermeasures equipment.

THIS AIRCRAFT IS ON LOAN FROM THE NATIONAL MUSEUM OF NAVAL AVIATION

Douglas Aircraft's famed designer Ed Heinemann designed the Navy A4D *Skyhawk* to replace the propeller driven AD-5 *Skyraider*. It was built small so that more could be accommodated on a carrier, where it excelled as the lightweight high-speed bomber for the U.S. Navy and Marines. It is a maneuverable, powerful, attack bomber with great altitude and range capabilities, plus an unusual flexibility in armament capacity. The small plane bucked the trend to 'bigger is better'; it offered a powerful punch, serving as the Navy's primary light bomber in the Vietnam era. One of its advantages in carrier service is its delta wing was so compact it didn't require a folding mechanism.

Fleet delivery began in September 1957. The A4Ds were redesignated as A-4s in 1962. The *Skyhawk*'s combat career began when it became the first American carrier-launched aircraft to raid North Vietnam on August 4, 1964. The aircraft would see heavy combat throughout the war. Senator John McCain would be shot down while piloting one over Hanoi and spend five years as a P.O.W. The later A-4F *Skyhawk II* served as the aircraft for the famous U.S. Navy Blue Angels flight demonstration team from 1974 to 1986.

A total of 638 night/all-weather capable A4D-2N Skyhawks (A-4C after 1962) were manufactured. Our aircraft, BuNo 148503 was built in El Segundo, California as the 348th of this variant. A total of 2,960 A-4s of all variants were produced.

The Museum's A-4 flew with the Navy in Southeast Asia, remaining active through the 1970s. In the late 1980s the plane was transferred to the Naval Air Maintenance Training Detachment School in Memphis, TN. There it served as a training aid for Naval Aviation specialists.

The aircraft was acquired by the Aerospace Museum in 2006. The aircraft is painted to represent the "Blue Angels" number "1" airplane, flown by the team Commander. Volunteers from the Aerospace Museum of California restored this aircraft in 2006 and again in 2022.

ATTACK BOMBER-Vietnam

VOUGHT A-7D
CORSAIR II

SPECIFICATIONS:

Crew: Pilot
Power plant: One 14,500 lb. thrust (64,500 newtons) Allison TF-41-A-1 turbofan.
Dimensions:
Span: 38 ft 9 in. (11.8 m)
Length: 46 ft 1-1/2 in. (14.06 m)
Height: 16 ft 0 in. (4.88 m)
Weight: Empty - 19,490 lbs. (8,840 Kg); Gross - 42,000 lbs. (19,050 Kg)
Performance:
Max. Speed: 698 mph (1,132 km/h) at low level.
Ferry range: over 4,000 miles (6,437 km).
Armament:
One fixed M-61 20 mm Vulcan cannon, two fuselage and six wing weapons stations with total combined capacity of 20,000 lbs. (Maximum external load: 15,000 lbs.)

THIS AIRCRAFT IS ON LOAN FROM THE NATIONAL MUSEUM OF THE USAF

A USAF decision to procure the Vought A-7 aircraft was the second instance in the decade of the 1960s to buy a Navy aircraft. The aircraft was modified to meet Air Force requirements by replacing the original Pratt & Whitney TF30 engine with a version of the Rolls-Royce Spay built in the US by Allison. The resulting TF-41-A-1 turbofan, increased power by 2,000 lb. (8,897 newtons) thrust and was much more efficient than the earlier engines. Other changes included installation of a 20 mm multi-barrel cannon, and advanced navigation/attack systems, heads-up display, and laser rangefinder. The Corsair II was developed for the US Navy as a replacement for their Douglas A-4 Light Attack aircraft. A total of 1,545 were built.

USAF S/N 70-0998 is an A-7D-8-CV, one of 450 A-7s built by Ling-Temco Vought in Dallas, Texas for the USAF. This aircraft was last assigned to the 156th Tactical Fighter Group (ANG), Puerto Rico, in 1990. Later that year it was flown to McClellan AFB for engineering evaluation. It was assigned to the museum in August 1992. It is displayed as received from the 156th Tactical Fighter Group.

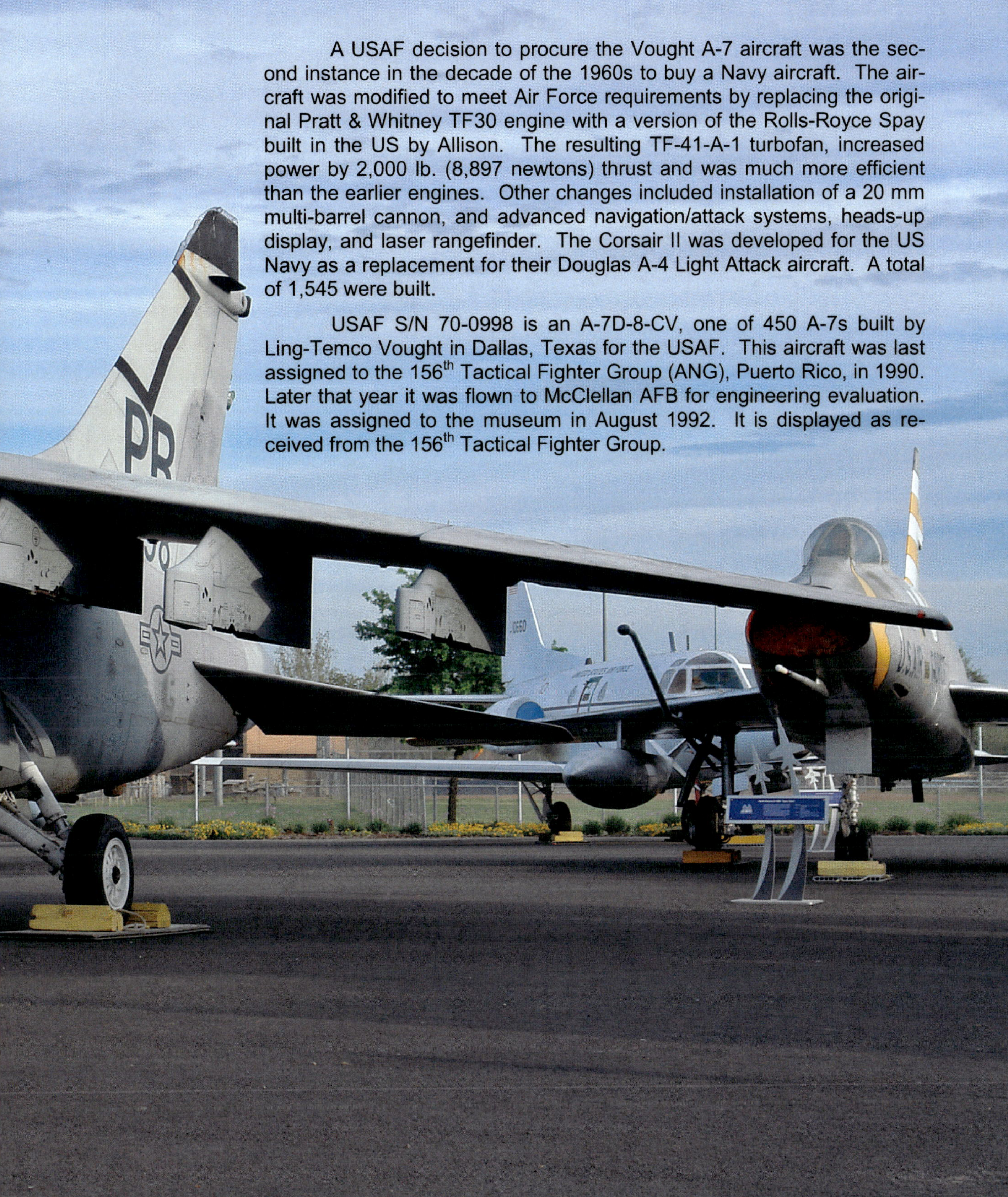

FAIRCHILD-REPUBLIC A-10A *THUNDERBOLT II* *(WARTHOG)*

SPECIFICATIONS:

Crew: Pilot

Power Plants: Two General Electric TF34-GE-100 turbofans, rated at 9,065 lb. thrust.

Dimensions:

Span:	57 ft 6 in.
Length:	53 ft 4 in.
Height:	14 ft 8 in.
Weight: Empty	20,246 lb.
Maximum Gross -	47,400 lbs.

Performance:

Speed: Maximum -	518 mph.
Range:	2,647 miles.

THIS AIRCRAFT IS ON LOAN FROM THE NATIONAL MUSEUM OF THE USAF

Fairchild-Republic A-10A was designed to kill tanks. The A-10 first flew in 1972. Two General Electric TF34-GE-100 high-bypass-ratio turbofan engines provide reliable thrust in the low altitude environment. Its weapons include a GE GAU-8/A "Avenger" 30-mm seven-barrel cannon, and the capability to carry up to 8 tons of external weapons on eight under-wing and three centerline pylons. Designed to counter the threat in the 1980s of the massive Soviet numerical superiority in tanks in Europe, the design incorporated many features to ensure its survivability. Although relatively slow, maximum speed of 400 knots, it could fly long distances, remain on station a very long time and employ a large number of various weapons. The aircraft saw its first combat during Operation Desert Storm in 1991 where it verified its reputation and also was used extensively to provide long-range air cover for search and rescue of downed aircrews. Efforts to retire the A-10A and AO-10A (Attack and Forward Air Control) have been reversed and extensive navigation systems, night warfare capabilities and more reliable electronics have been added to keep the airplanes in the active force.

USAF S/N 76-540 is an A-10A, one of 713 built by Fairchild-Republic at Hagerstown, Maryland. It was delivered to the 354th Tactical Fighter Wing (TAC), Myrtle Beach AFB, South Carolina in 1978. In August 1983 it was sent to the 706th TAC Fighter Squadron (AFRES), NAS New Orleans, Louisiana. During an Operation Desert Storm mission on January 31, 1991, the aircraft suffered major damage when struck by a surface-to-air missile. Although all hydraulic controls were lost, the pilot, Major Jim Rose, managed to bring it home using backup systems. After repairs, it was flown to McClellan on August 22, 1991 to supply parts to other A-10s before being retired to the museum.

COMPOSITE ENGINEERING INC
BQM-167
SKEETER

SPECIFICATIONS:

Crew:	Unmanned, remotely controlled
Power Plant:	One Microturbo TRI 60-5 jet engine, 1,000 lb. thrust
Dimensions:	
Span:	10 ft 6 in.
Length:	20 ft 1 in.
Height:	4 ft 5 in.
Weight: Gross -	2,050 lbs.
Performance:	
Speed:	714 mph (Mach .93)
Altitude:	50 feet to 51,000 feet
Maneuverability:	-2g to 9g
Range:	3+ hours
Armament:	None

THIS AIRCRAFT IS ON LOAN FROM CEI, Sacramento, CA

Composite Engineering, Inc., CEI, is a Sacramento, California aerospace firm specializing in providing unmanned high performance aerial vehicles suitable for use as aerial targets. These vehicles are being provided to the US Military and selected international customers where they are flown aggressively to simulate aerial threats that air defense crews might face in combat.

As a current production aircraft the BQM-167 utilizes the latest carbon fiber composite technologies in its construction, along with the latest in command and control systems. It is launched from the ground using a solid rocket motor to achieve flying speed. Once launched the rocket falls away and the Tri 60-5 jet engine provides 1000 pounds of thrust, sufficient to fly at speeds in excess of .91 Mach and altitudes up to 51,000 feet. Unrefueled missions can last for over 3 hours. At the end of the mission the vehicle is recovered using a self-contained parachute.

NORTHROP MQM-36B *SHELDUCK*

SPECIFICATIONS:

Crew:	Unmanned, remotely controlled
Powerplant:	One McCulloch O-100-2, 90 hp, 4 cylinder air-cooled engine.
Dimensions:	
Wingspan:	11 ft 6 in (3.5 m)
Length:	12 ft 8 in (3.86 m)
Height:	2 ft 6 in (0.76 m)
Weight: Gross	360 lbs. (163.3 kg)
Empty	271 lbs. (122.9 kg)
Performance:	
Maximum speed:	230 mph (370 km/h)
Service ceiling:	23,000 ft (7,000 m)
Endurance:	1 hour
Production:	73,000 of all variants built from 1948 to 1966.

OWNED BY THE AEROSPACE MUSEUM OF CALIFORNIA

The MQM-36 target drone began life in the late 1940s, evolving through a series of refinements with the US Army designations of OQ-19A through D, and the US Navy name of *Quail* with designations of KD2R-1 through 5. These drones were designed by the Radioplane Corporation, which was later acquired by Northrop Aviation. In 1962 it received the designation MQM-36 in the joint aircraft nomenclature system.

Although initially used to train anti-aircraft gunners, it was later used with hand-held guided missiles such as the *Stinger*. It is launched from a zero-length rail either on land or aboard a ship with the aid of a rocket booster attached below the rear of its body. It is then remotely flown by an operator within line-of-sight. Machine guns, cannon and missiles are used in an attempt to shoot it down. If it survives its mission, it can be recovered by deploying a parachute housed in the top of the fuselage. It is then recovered by a helicopter that lifts the drone by a cable attached to the ring at the end of its tail. It is then refurbished in preparation for its next sortie.

The pods on the wing tips contain radar reflectors to simulate the electronic signature of a much larger aircraft.

The aircraft was donated to the Aerospace Museum of California by Jeffery Travis Parker.

LOCKHEED F-80B *SHOOTING STAR*

SPECIFICATIONS:

Crew:	One- Pilot
Power Plant:	One Allison J-33-A-11, Thrust, 4,000 lb. (17,793 newtons)
Dimensions:	
Span:	38 ft 9 in. (11.8 m)
Length:	34 ft 5 in. (10.5 m)
Height:	11 ft 3 in. (3.4 m)
Weight:	Empty 8,420 lbs. (3,819 kg)
	Gross - 16,856 lbs. (7,644 kg)
Performance:	
Speed, Maximum:	558 mph (898 km/h)
Range:	1,200 miles (1,931 km)

Armament: six .50 cal. MG in nose. Could carry up to four 1,000 lb bombs and four 5" HVAR rockets.

THIS AIRCRAFT IS ON LOAN FROM THE NATIONAL MUSEUM OF THE USAF

Built by Lockheed Aircraft, the F-80 was the first American jet fighter placed in operational service by the Air Force, and the first to exceed 500 mph in level flight. The prototype XP-80 aircraft first flew on January 8, 1944. The designation was changed to F-80 in June 1948. Although originally designed as an interceptor, the F-80C model saw extensive service during the Korean War as a fighter-bomber. In the first jet versus jet combat, an F-80C shot down a MiG-15 fighter.

USAF S/N 45-8704 was built as a P-80B-1-LO, one of 240 delivered by Lockheed Aircraft in Burbank, California. It was delivered to the USAF on January 29, 1948 and assigned to the 1st Fighter Group (TAC), March Field, California. In August 1949 it went to the 36th Fighter Group (USAFE), Furstenfeldbruck AB, Germany. In October 1950 it went to the 7540th Maintenance Group (USAFE), RAF Burtonwood, England; and then in September 1951, to the 3595th Pilot Training Wing (ATC), Williams AFB, Arizona. In December 1951 it was converted to F-80C-12-LO fighter-bomber configuration. In September 1953 it went to its last unit, the 185th Fighter Squadron (ANG), Will Rogers Field, Oklahoma. It was retired in July 1958, and obtained by the museum in July 1983.

It is currently painted in the markings of 23rd Fighter Squadron, 36th Fighter Group, 1948 period.

REPUBLIC F-84F
THUNDERSTREAK

SPECIFICATIONS:

Crew:	One Pilot
Power Plant: One Wright J65-W-3 "Sapphire", thrust 7,220 lb. (32,116 newtons)	
Dimensions:	
Span:	33 ft 6 in. (10.2 m)
Length:	43 ft 4 in. (13.2 m)
Height:	14 ft 4 in. (4.37 m)
Weight: Gross -	25,000 lbs. (11,338 kg)
Performance:	
Speed:	650 mph (1,046 km/h)
Combat Radius:	1,000 miles (1,609 km)
Service Ceiling:	over 45,000 ft (13,700 m)

Armament:

Six .50 cal. M/G, four in fuselage, two in wing root.
Provisions for carrying external stores including 24 - 5 in. rockets, or four 1,000 lb bombs, or tactical atomic stores.

THIS AIRCRAFT IS ON LOAN FROM THE NATIONAL MUSEUM OF THE USAF

Built by Republic Aircraft as a fighter-escort for Strategic Air Command bombers, and fighter-bomber and reconnaissance types for the Tactical Air Command; the swept wing F-84F and RF-84F replaced the F-84E and F-84G straight-wing models that served in the Korean War. The F-84F would see extensive service in NATO air forces in Europe through the 1950s and into the 1970s.

USAF S/N 51-1772 is an F-84F-30-RE, built by Republic Aviation in Farmingdale, New York, and delivered to the Air Force on October 5, 1954. It was first assigned to the 12th Strategic Fighter Wing (SAC), Bergstrom AFB, Texas; and was transferred to the 31st Strategic Fighter Wing (SAC), Turner AFB, Georgia in February, 1956. In August 1957 it went to the 119th Fighter Interceptor Squadron (ANG), McGuire AFB, New Jersey; moving later to the 12th Tactical Fighter Wing (TAC), McDill AFB, Florida in July 1962, and the 36th Tactical Fighter Group (TAC), Holloman AFB, New Mexico in March 1964, and the 104th Tactical Fighter Group (ANG), Barnes Field, Mass. in August 1965. It was retired to Davis-Monthan AFB, Arizona in August 1971 and shipped to the museum in February 1983.

NORTH AMERICAN F-86F *SABRE*

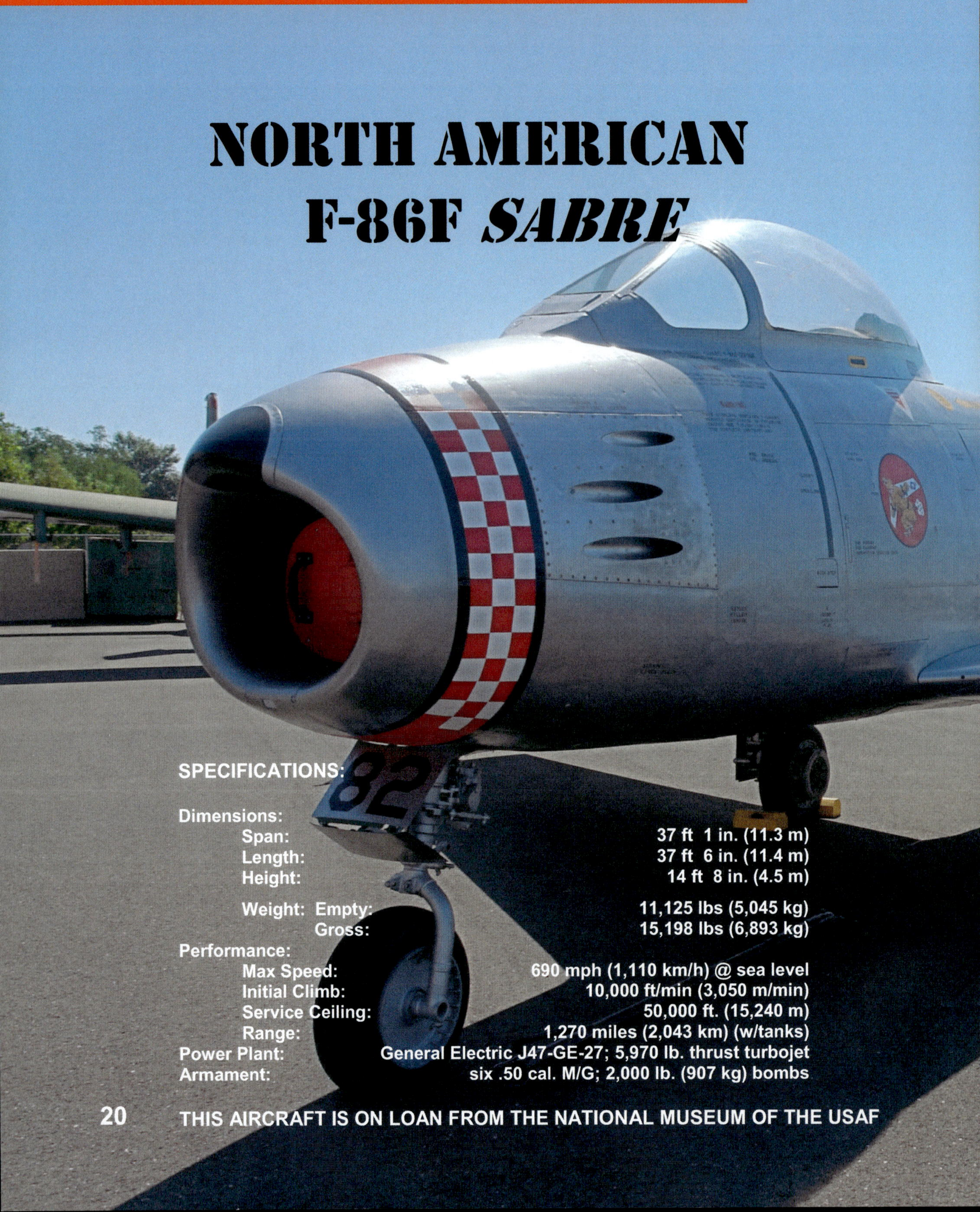

SPECIFICATIONS:

Dimensions:		
	Span:	37 ft 1 in. (11.3 m)
	Length:	37 ft 6 in. (11.4 m)
	Height:	14 ft 8 in. (4.5 m)
	Weight: Empty:	11,125 lbs (5,045 kg)
	Gross:	15,198 lbs (6,893 kg)
Performance:		
	Max Speed:	690 mph (1,110 km/h) @ sea level
	Initial Climb:	10,000 ft/min (3,050 m/min)
	Service Ceiling:	50,000 ft. (15,240 m)
	Range:	1,270 miles (2,043 km) (w/tanks)
Power Plant:		General Electric J47-GE-27; 5,970 lb. thrust turbojet
Armament:		six .50 cal. M/G; 2,000 lb. (907 kg) bombs

THIS AIRCRAFT IS ON LOAN FROM THE NATIONAL MUSEUM OF THE USAF

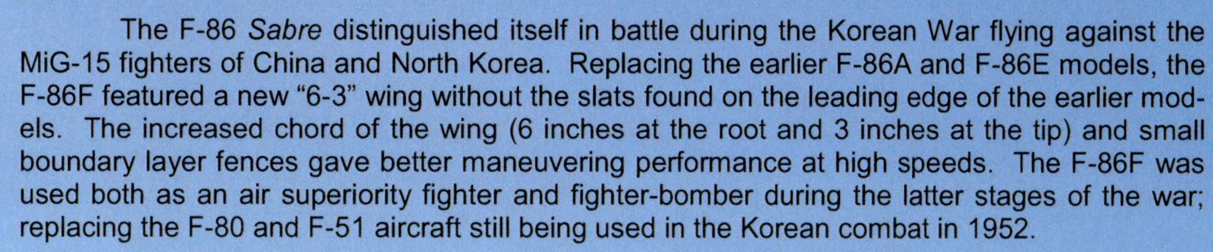

The F-86 *Sabre* distinguished itself in battle during the Korean War flying against the MiG-15 fighters of China and North Korea. Replacing the earlier F-86A and F-86E models, the F-86F featured a new "6-3" wing without the slats found on the leading edge of the earlier models. The increased chord of the wing (6 inches at the root and 3 inches at the tip) and small boundary layer fences gave better maneuvering performance at high speeds. The F-86F was used both as an air superiority fighter and fighter-bomber during the latter stages of the war; replacing the F-80 and F-51 aircraft still being used in the Korean combat in 1952.

USAF S/N 51-13082 is an F-86F-20-NH, built by North American Aviation in Columbus, Ohio and delivered to the 126th Fighter Interceptor Squadron (ADC), Madison, Wisconsin on September 5, 1952. In July, 1953 it went to the 18th Fighter Interceptor Squadron (ADC), Minneapolis, Minn., with other assignments being to the 49th Fighter Interceptor Squadron (ADC), Dow AFB, Maine in May, 1954; 3595th Combat Crew Training Wing (ATC), Nellis AFB, Nevada in December, 1954; 3525th Combat Crew Training Wing (ATC), Williams AFB, Arizona; 21st Fighter Interceptor Squadron (ANG), Andrews AFB, Maryland in May, 1957; and the 115th Fighter Interceptor Squadron (ANG), Van Nuys, California in October, 1957.

Its last unit of assignment was the 195th Fighter Interceptor Squadron (ANG), Van Nuys, California in April 1959. The aircraft was retired in October 1959 and loaned to AMVETS Post 55 in Goleta, California. It was transported to the museum in April 1986.

Our aircraft is displayed in the colors of the 195th Fighter Squadron, California Air National Guard.

NORTH AMERICAN F-86L "DOG" SABRE

SPECIFICATIONS:

Crew:	One Pilot
Dimensions:	
Span:	39 ft 1 in. (11.9 m)
Length:	41 ft. (12.5 m)
Height:	14 ft. (4.3 m)
Weight: Max -	16,500 lbs. (7,483 kg)
Performance:	
Max. Speed:	670 mph (1,078 km/h)
Service Ceiling:	53,000 ft. (15,240 m)
Tactical Radius:	535 miles (860 km)

Power Plant: One General Electric J47-GE-27, thrust 5,970 lb. (26,555 newtons)

Armament: Twenty-four 2.75 inch unguided rockets carried in an internal tray in fuselage.

THIS AIRCRAFT IS ON LOAN FROM THE NATIONAL MUSEUM OF THE USAF

Built by North American Aviation as a radar guided, rocket armed, all-weather fighter-interceptor derived from the F-86 *Sabre* of Korean War fame. Originally designated the F-86D, the aircraft underwent modifications to upgrade the original radar/fire control systems to provide “data-link” capability between the aircraft and ground controllers, eliminating the use of vocal instructions during intercept missions. New wing slats and an increase in wing span of 2 feet improved performance of the F-86L over the F-86D. The nickname “Dog Sabre” derived from the “D” version’s sub-type letter and it radome that resembled a dog’s snout.

USAF S/N 51-02968 was built as an F-86D-20-NA by North American Aviation in Inglewood, California, and delivered to the Air Force on April 22, 1953. It was first sent to the 97th Fighter Interceptor Squadron (ADC), Wright-Patterson AFB, Ohio. In March 1955 it went to the 3555th Combat Crew Training Wing (ATC), Perrin AFB, Texas. It was sent to Fresno, California for modification to an F-86L in February 1957. In November 1959 it went to the 124th Fighter Interceptor Group (ANG), Boise, Idaho where it remained until retired in April 1964. The aircraft was obtained by a rancher in Texas, who donated it to the museum in 1983.

NORTH AMERICAN F-100D
SUPER SABRE

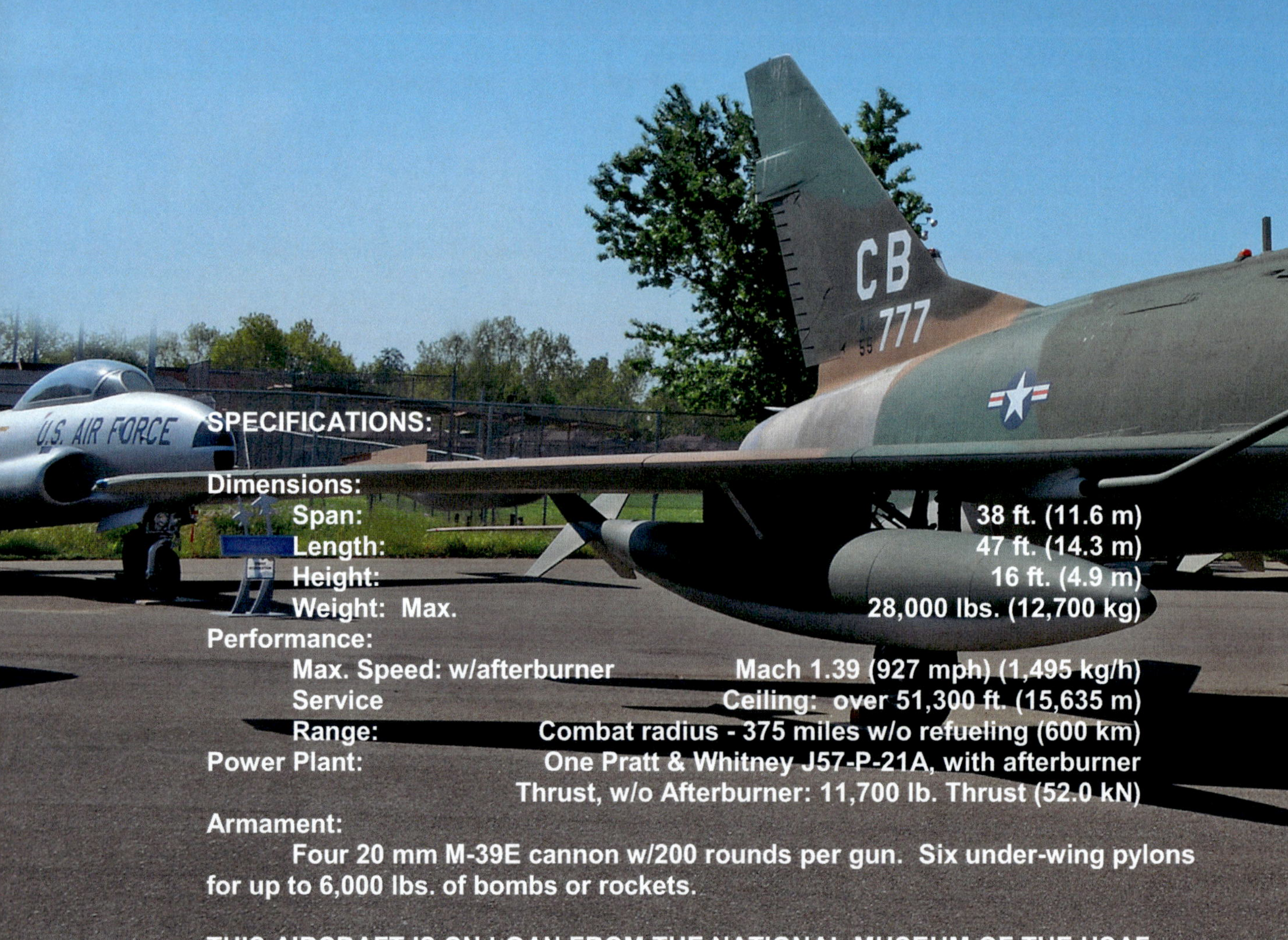

SPECIFICATIONS:

Dimensions:	
Span:	38 ft. (11.6 m)
Length:	47 ft. (14.3 m)
Height:	16 ft. (4.9 m)
Weight: Max.	28,000 lbs. (12,700 kg)
Performance:	
Max. Speed: w/afterburner	Mach 1.39 (927 mph) (1,495 kg/h)
Service	Ceiling: over 51,300 ft. (15,635 m)
Range:	Combat radius - 375 miles w/o refueling (600 km)
Power Plant:	One Pratt & Whitney J57-P-21A, with afterburner
	Thrust, w/o Afterburner: 11,700 lb. Thrust (52.0 kN)

Armament:

Four 20 mm M-39E cannon w/200 rounds per gun. Six under-wing pylons for up to 6,000 lbs. of bombs or rockets.

THIS AIRCRAFT IS ON LOAN FROM THE NATIONAL MUSEUM OF THE USAF

Built by North American Aviation, this was the world's first production supersonic aircraft. It served as a fighter-bomber during the Vietnam War; and was used by the USAF "*Thunderbirds*" for many years. It is equipped with an aerial refueling boom under the right wing. The family resemblance to the earlier F-86 *Sabrejet* is apparent, but the performance with the afterburning engine is significantly enhanced.

The museums aircraft is a F-100D, USAF S/N 56-3288, and was built in Inglewood, California. It was assigned to the 493rd Tactical Fighter Squadron, 48th Tactical Fighter Wing (USAFE), first at Toul-Rosieres AB, France, then at Lakenheath AB, England. In March 1972 it went to the 131st Tactical Fighter Group (ANG), St. Louis, Missouri. It was retired to Davis-Monthan AFB, Arizona in December 1975, and flown to the museum in 1983.

A total of 2,294 F-100s were built, of which 1,274 were F-100Ds. Although built as a fighter, the airplane was never credited with an aerial victory. However, it excelled as a fighter-bomber in Viet Nam where *Super Sabres* flew 360,283 combat sorties, a number that exceeded the total number of combat sorties flown by 15,000-plus P-51 *Mustangs* in World War II.

The aircraft has recently been repainted as F-100D-41-NH, S/N 55-3777 to reflect the appearance of the hundreds of F-100s that served in Vietnam. S/N 55-3777 was an aircraft of the 90th TFS/3rd TFW stationed at Bein Hoa AB, Vietnam in 1969, where its primary pilot was Jack Doub. He had obtained sponsorship from the Riviera Casino in Las Vegas, and named the airplane *"Miss Riviera"*. It then operated with the 35th TFW stationed at Phan Rang until January 1970 when it was lost due to engine oil system failure during takeoff. Tail Codes were used throughout the USAF as a way to identify the squadron to which an aircraft was assigned. The "CB" on the tail identifies the airplane as being assigned to the 90th Tactical Fighter Squadron.

MCDONNELL F-101B
VOODOO

SPECIFICATIONS:

Crew: two
Power Plants: Two Pratt & Whitney J57-P-55, 11,990 lbt (53.3 kN) thrust turbojets, with Afterburner, 16,900 lbt (75.2 kN)
Dimensions:
- Span: 39 ft 8 in. (12.1 m)
- Length: 67 ft 5 in. (20.5 m)
- Height: 18 ft. (5.5 m)
- Weight: 28,495 lb (12,923 kg) Empty, 52,400 lb (23,764 kg) Max

Performance:
- Speed: 1,134 mph at 35,000 ft. (1,825 km/h)
- Range: 1,520 miles (2,446 km)

Armament:
- Three AIM-4D Falcon missiles internal.
- Two AIR-2A Genie missiles w/nuclear warheads external.
- MG-13 Fire control system with automatic search and track mode.

 THIS AIRCRAFT IS ON LOAN FROM THE NATIONAL MUSEUM OF THE USAF

Produced by McDonnell Aircraft Co., the F-101 was the first USAF fighter capable of over 1,000 mph in level flight. Originally designed as a long-range escort fighter, it was produced in two configurations: air defense fighter (F-101B), and reconnaissance (RF-101A). The F-101B first flew on March 27, 1957.

USAF S/N 57-427 is an F-101B-100-MC, one of 407 F-101Bs built by McDonnell Aircraft in St. Louis, Missouri. It was delivered to the Air Force on February 29, 1960 and assigned to the 52nd Fighter Group (ADC), Suffolk County AFB, New York. In November 1969 it was transferred to the 101st Fighter Group (ANG), Dow AFB, Maine, and then in August 1978 to the 147th Fighter Interceptor Group (ANG), Ellington AFB, Texas. It was flown to the museum on May 5, 1982.

CONVAIR F-102A
DELTA DAGGER

SPECIFICATIONS:

Crew: One.
Power Plant: One Pratt & Whitney J57-P-23, w/afterburner; 17,000 lb (75.6 kN) thrust.
Dimensions:

Span:	38 ft 1-1/2 in. (11.6 m)
Length:	68 ft 3 in. (20.8 m)
Height:	21 ft 2-1/2 in. (6.46 m)
Weight: Empty	19,350 lb (8,775 kg)
Loaded	24,500 lb (11,111 kg)

Performance: Max. Speed 825 mph (1,328 km/h) (Mach 1.2) at 36,000 ft.
Armament:
Six Hughes GAR-1D or -2A Falcon missiles mounted on rails in fuselage.
Provision for twenty-four 2.75 in. rockets in firing channels in missile bay doors.

THIS AIRCRAFT IS ON LOAN FROM THE NATIONAL MUSEUM OF THE USAF

Built by Convair (General Dynamics) the F-102 was the first all-weather supersonic jet interceptor. Its supersonic capability is a result of its being the first adapted to use the "area rule" design concept. Note the contoured rear fuselage, which reduces high speed drag. The F-102 was superseded by the more advanced and powerful F-106, which could exceed 1,000 mph. Both aircraft feature delta shaped wings, which eliminate the need for conventional horizontal control surfaces (stabilizer and elevators).

USAF S/N 56-1140 is an F-102A-65-CO, one of 875 F-102As built by Convair in San Diego, California. It was delivered to the USAF on June 4, 1957 and assigned to the 438th Fighter Interceptor Squadron (ADC), Kinrose AFB, Michigan. In March 1958 it went to the 95th Fighter Interceptor Squadron (ADC), Andrews AFB, Maryland, and then in February 1960 to the 509th Fighter Interceptor Squadron, Clark AB, Philippines. Its last assignment was with the 154th Fighter Group (ANG), Hickam AFB, Hawaii beginning in January 1957. It was flown to the museum in a C-5 transport on October 7, 1984.

It is displayed in the colors of the 431st Fighter Interceptor Squadron "Red Devils", and carries tail number 55-431 in honor of that unit, which was assigned to a test squadron at McClellan AFB for many years.

LOCKHEED F-104B *STARFIGHTER*

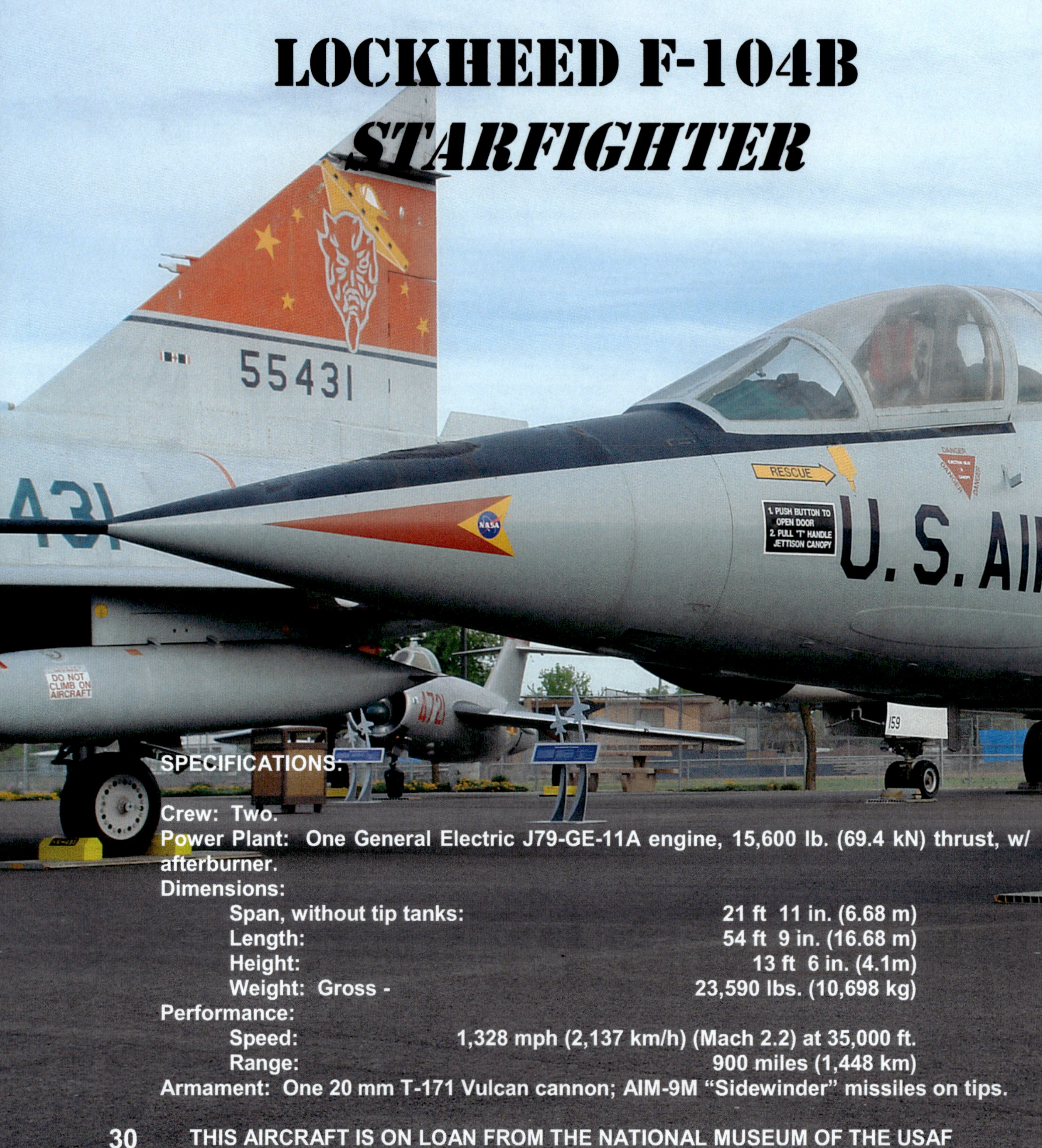

SPECIFICATIONS:

Crew: Two.
Power Plant: One General Electric J79-GE-11A engine, 15,600 lb. (69.4 kN) thrust, w/ afterburner.
Dimensions:

Span, without tip tanks:	21 ft 11 in. (6.68 m)
Length:	54 ft 9 in. (16.68 m)
Height:	13 ft 6 in. (4.1m)
Weight: Gross -	23,590 lbs. (10,698 kg)

Performance:

Speed:	1,328 mph (2,137 km/h) (Mach 2.2) at 35,000 ft.
Range:	900 miles (1,448 km)

Armament: One 20 mm T-171 Vulcan cannon; AIM-9M "Sidewinder" missiles on tips.

THIS AIRCRAFT IS ON LOAN FROM THE NATIONAL MUSEUM OF THE USAF

Built by Lockheed as a Mach 2+ interceptor and air superiority fighter, the F-104 was unique in several respects. With its exceptionally thin and small wing span of only 21 feet, low speed lift was generated by blowing air from the engine over the upper wing surface. The F-104B is a two-seat trainer and combat aircraft. NASA used ours as a test flight "chase" aircraft. A variety of models of the aircraft were built under license as part of the Military Assistance Program, and flew with air forces in Canada, Belgium, Germany, Pakistan, and Japan. In total, 2,578 F-104 series aircraft were built. Later models were equipped with a retractable probe for in-flight refueling, improving the range that was otherwise limited as all fuel had to be carried either in the fuselage or on external drop tanks.

The General Electric J79 afterburning turbojet engine powers the F-104, with air entering by the side-mounted fixed intakes. These are non-variable, and optimized for speeds in excess of Mach 2. High temperatures, created by air friction on the aluminum airframe, not engine thrust or airframe drag, limit the top speed of the *Starfighter*.

USAF S/N 57-1303 is an F-104B-10-LO, one of only 26 built by Lockheed Aircraft in Burbank, California. It was delivered to the Air Force on October 2, 1958, and handed over to NASA in December 1959. Based at Edwards AFB, California, it was the only F-104B that NASA operated, and it carried the registration N819NA. It was used to train pilots on how to land the X-15 and Space Shuttle, along with use as a "chase" aircraft. Many famous aviators have flown N819NA, including Neil Armstrong and Chuck Yeager. It was flown to the museum in a C-130 on July 13, 1983.

REPUBLIC F-105D *THUNDERCHIEF*

SPECIFICATIONS:

Crew:		**One Pilot**
Power Plant:	**Pratt & Whitney J75-P-19W turbojet, thrust 24,500 lb. (108.9 kN)**	
Dimensions:		
Span:		**34 ft 11 in. (10.6 m)**
Length:		**64 ft 3 in. (19.6 m)**
Height:		**19 ft 8 in. (6.0 m)**
Weigh: Maximum -		**52,550 lbs. (23,832 kg)**
Performance:		
Speed: Max -		**1,390 mph (2,237 km/h), (Mach 2.25) at 36,000 ft.**
Ceiling:		**52,000 ft. (15,850 m)**
Range: w/o refueling -		**2,000 miles (3,220 km)**
Armament:	**One 20 mm GE Vulcan cannon. Up to 8,000 lbs of other weapons.**	

THIS AIRCRAFT IS ON LOAN FROM THE NATIONAL MUSEUM OF THE USAF

Built by Republic Aircraft, the F-105 was designed as a supersonic single seat fighter-bomber able to carry nuclear weapons and heavy bomb loads over great distances at high speeds. The aircraft made its first flight on October 12, 1955. The F-105D was the all-weather fighter-bomber version, fitted with a 20mm "Gatling-type" gun, a Doppler radar for night or bad weather operations and external fuel tanks. The original weapons bay was designed for nuclear stores but was routinely used for additional fuel tanks. Bombs, rockets and other weapons were carried externally on the centerline of the fuselage, or on wing pylons. The aircraft was fitted with a retractable in-flight refueling probe. During the Vietnam War F-105 units carried-out the major bombing operations in the high-threat areas of North Vietnam, known as Route Package VI, flying from bases at Tahkli and Korat in Thailand. The Thunderchief was reputable for its very high speed capabilities at very low altitude and was considered the best fighter-bomber in the Vietnam War.

USAF S/N 62-4301 is an F-105D-31-RE, one of 610 F-105Ds built by Republic Aviation in Farmingdale, New York. It was delivered to the USAF on April 25, 1963 and assigned to the 8th Tactical Fighter Wing (PACAF), Itazuke AB, Japan. In May 1964 it was assigned to the 41st Air Division (PACAF), at Yokota AB, Japan, where it was stationed until January 1968 when it was sent to the 18th Tactical Fighter Wing (PACAF), Osan AB, Korea. While with the 18th TFW it made two brief combat tours with the 355th TFW at Takhli AB, Thailand, and achieved an unofficial ground kill of an IL-28 bomber during one of the tours. From April to August 1972 it was here at McClellan for maintenance. It then went to the 507th Tactical Fighter Group (AFRES), Tinker AFB, Oklahoma, and finally in July 1980 to the 466th Tactical Fighter Squadron (AFRES), Hill AFB, Utah. It was flown to the museum on January 16, 1984.

CONVAIR F-106A
DELTA DART

SPECIFICATIONS:

Crew: One pilot
Production: 277 F-106As, 63 F-106Bs
Mission – Interceptor: Primary - Strategic Defense
Secondary - Aerial Supremacy
Power Plant: One Pratt & Whitney J75-P17, thrust 16,100 lbs (71.6 kN)
Thrust, in afterburner 24,500 lbs (108.9 kN)
Dimensions:
Wing Span: 38 ft 4 in. (11.7 m)
Length: 70 ft 9in. (21.6 m)
Height: 20 ft 4 in. (6.2 m)
Weight: Gross, Empty – 24,861 lbs. (11,275 kg)
Maximum – 41,831 lbs. (18,970 kg)
Performance:
Speed: Maximum – Mach 2.4 at 40,000 ft, Mach 1.1 at Sea Level, .93 Mach Cruise.
Ceiling: 56,000 ft. (17,070 m)
Combat radius: 735 miles (1,183 km)
Armament: Two AIM4F Radar Missiles, Two AIM 4G Infrared Missiles, One AIR2A(1.5KT) *Genie* Nuclear Rocket, or one M61 Gating-type 20 mm cannon with 450 rounds.

THIS AIRCRAFT IS ON LOAN FROM THE NATIONAL MUSEUM OF THE USAF

The single seat, single engine, delta-wing, Mach 2, F-106 *Delta Dart* fighter interceptor was the cornerstone of the strategic air defense of the United States from 1959 through 1987. Designed to intercept and destroy the Soviet bomber threat in the Cold War, the *Delta Dart* carried sophisticated radar and infrared missiles, including a nuclear tipped rocket to defeat attacking fleets of bombers. Later a six-barrel 20 mm Gatling-type machine gun replaced the rocket as the F-106 was deployed worldwide to counter possible threats from fighters.

Equipped as an all-weather, day or night fighter, the *Dart* used encrypted data link and a computer-controlled radar fire control system to find, track, lock-on and destroy an adversary aircraft regardless of electronic counter-counter measures, jamming, or decoy processes. The F-106 was considered the most challenging of fighters to fly due to its heavy cockpit workload.

Today, the F-106 still holds the record as the fastest single engine fighter in the world, having achieved over 1525 miles per hour. The *Delta Dart* could snap climb to over 65,000 feet. Internal armament and special supersonic tanks allowed the F-106 to achieve a combat radius of over 700 miles and without refueling. One example flew 2075 miles non-stop. Its unique Coke bottle shape and delta wing design proved the F-106 to be highly maneuverable and it was used in the adversary role against the Navy Top Gun School and as simulated enemy forces at Red Flag Exercises.

Painted in its original assigned colors of the 5th Fighter Squadron, aircraft 59-0010 survived a mid-air collision where it lost the first 14 feet of its nose. Its last assignment was to be towed by a C-141 to test the feasibility of launching satellites from its internal bay into space. The Sacramento Air Logistics Center was the assigned repair depot for the F-106 and processed virtually all F-106s from 1959 through to 1985. Volunteers from the Aerospace Museum of California restored this aircraft in 2005/6.

GENERAL DYNAMICS FB-111A
AARDVARK

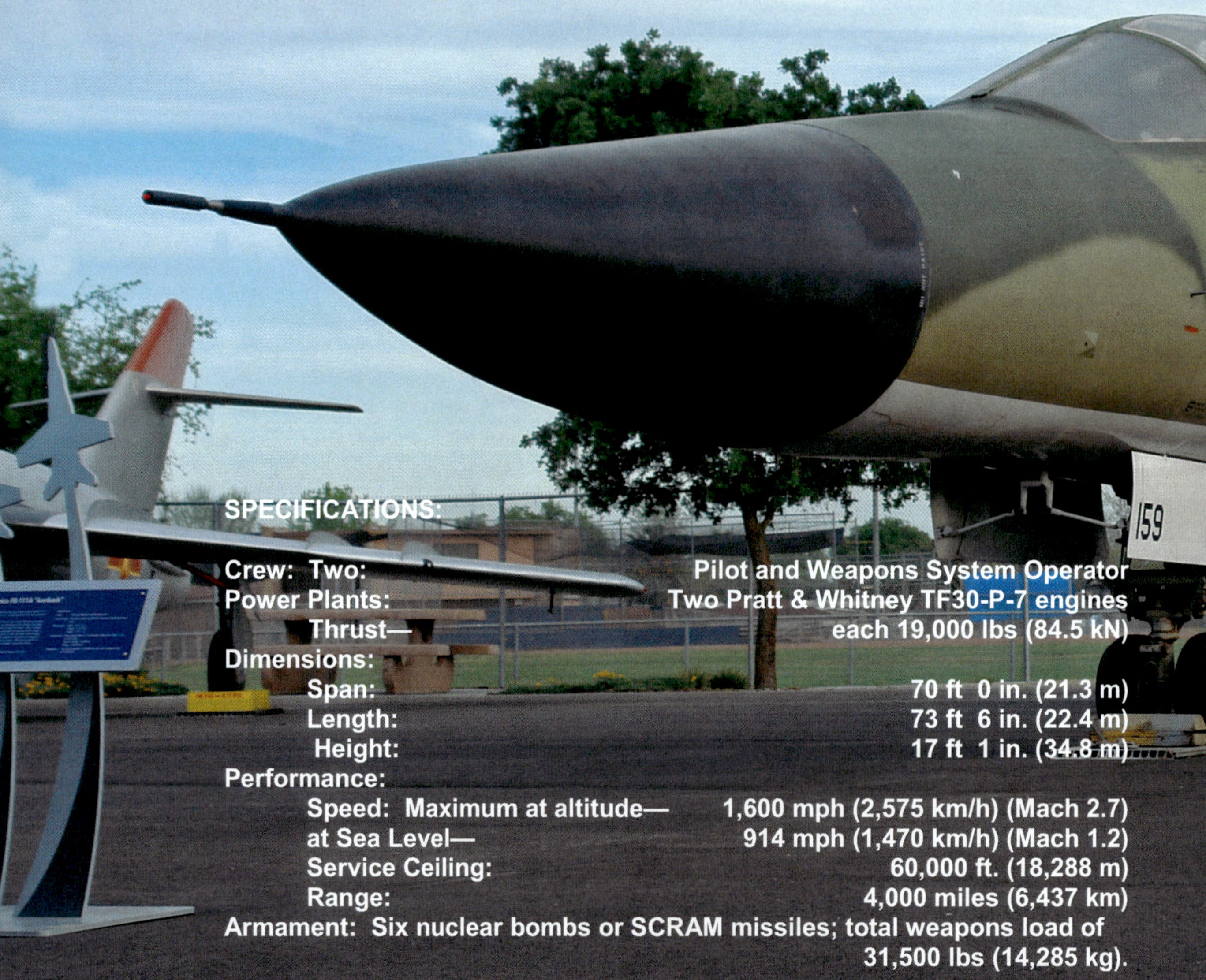

SPECIFICATIONS:

Crew: Two: Pilot and Weapons System Operator
Power Plants: Two Pratt & Whitney TF30-P-7 engines
Thrust— each 19,000 lbs (84.5 kN)
Dimensions:
Span: 70 ft 0 in. (21.3 m)
Length: 73 ft 6 in. (22.4 m)
Height: 17 ft 1 in. (34.8 m)
Performance:
Speed: Maximum at altitude— 1,600 mph (2,575 km/h) (Mach 2.7)
at Sea Level— 914 mph (1,470 km/h) (Mach 1.2)
Service Ceiling: 60,000 ft. (18,288 m)
Range: 4,000 miles (6,437 km)
Armament: Six nuclear bombs or SCRAM missiles; total weapons load of 31,500 lbs (14,285 kg).

THIS AIRCRAFT IS ON LOAN FROM THE NATIONAL MUSEUM OF THE USAF

Developed as a medium-range bomber for the Strategic Air Command, the FB-111 is based upon the F-111 fighter, which was the first production aircraft to utilize the variable-sweep wing, incorporate automatic terrain-following radar, and feature a crew module escape capsule. Originally planned to replace the B-52C/F versions of the *Stratofortress*. Compared to the F-111 the wingspan of the FB-111 was lengthened, its landing gear strengthened, and braking increased. Provisions were made to carry six nuclear bombs, or six SRAM missiles, or a combination of these weapons. The F-111 never received an official nickname. It was called the *Aadvark* by its crews because its long nose resembled that animal.

The F-111 "swing" wing is a feature allowing relatively low landing speeds and excellent range, while at the same time being able to sprint to more than twice the speed of sound. The F-111 had various variants including the TAC F-111D and the Australian export version, the F-111C. The last remaining operational F-111 aircraft were those in service with the Royal Australian Air Force. These were retired in December 2010 after 43 years of front line service.

USAF S/N 67-159 is an FB-111A-CF, the first of 76 built by General Dynamics in Fort Worth, Texas. It was delivered to the USAF on September 4, 1968 and assigned to the Air Force Flight Test Center (AFSC), Edwards AFB, California. In July 1980 it was assigned to the Sacramento Air Logistics Center (AFLC), McClellan AFB, California to test and verify technological and weapons modifications. Originally painted in the white and orange of Sacramento Flight Test, It was retired in August 1990, and is painted in the camouflaged color scheme used by strategic and tactical forces.

MCDONNELL-DOUGLAS F-4C
PHANTOM II

SPECIFICATIONS:

Crew:		Two
Power Plants:		Two General Electric J79-GE-15
Thrust, each		17,500 lb. (77.8 kN)
Dimensions:		
Span:		38 ft 7-1/2 in. (11.8 m)
Length:		63 ft 0 in. (19.2 m)
Height:		16 ft 5-1/2 in. (5.0 m)
Weight:	Empty	30,328 lbs (9,244 kg)
	Maximum Takeoff -	61,795 lbs (18,835 kg)
Performance:		
Speed:		1,600 mph (2,575 km/h) at 36,000 ft.

Armament:

Can carry over 16,000 lbs (7,256 kg) of ordnance, including missiles, bombs, 20 mm gun pod, etc.

THIS AIRCRAFT IS ON LOAN FROM THE NATIONAL MUSEUM OF THE USAF

Built by McDonnell Aircraft as a twin-engine, two-seat, long-range, all-weather interceptor and attack bomber for the Navy, the F-4 was adopted by the Air Force to replace the F-105. The USAF F-4C first flew on May 27, 1963. The aircrafts unique aerodynamic design incorporates "the coke bottle " fuselage, downward shaped elevons, and upward sloped outer wings. Raw thrust from the two engines gave it a reputation for rapid acceleration. Two squadrons of F-4Cs were later modified as "Wild Weasel" aircraft which incorporated sophisticated electronics to counter enemy surface to air missiles. 5,195 Phantom IIs were produced by McDonnell Aircraft Company, making it the second most produced and exported American jet fighter, after the North American F-86 Sabre. The aircraft has been operated by the USAF, US Navy, US Marines, eleven foreign nations, and for a time used by both the USAF Thunderbirds and USN Blue Angels.

USAF S/N 64-706 is an F-4C-22-MC, one of 583 F-4Cs built in St. Louis, Missouri. It was delivered to the USAF on May 12, 1965 and assigned to the 366th Tactical Fighter Wing (TAC), Holloman AFB, New Mexico. In January 1966 it was sent to the 12th Tactical Fighter Wing (PACAF), Cam Ranh Bay, Vietnam for a two year combat tour. In April 1968 it went to the 479th Tactical Fighter Wing (TAC), George AFB, California. The final two assignments were to the 58th Tactical Fighter Wing (TAC), Luke AFB, Arizona in August 1974, and the 191st Fighter Interceptor Group (ANG), Selfridge AFB, Michigan. It was flown to the museum on July 22, 1986 bearing the black and yellow checkerboard of the Selfridge Fighter Squadron.

GRUMMAN F-14D
TOMCAT

SPECIFICATIONS:

Crew:	Two - Pilot and Weapons Officer (RO)
Power Plant:	Two General Electric F110-GE-400 turbofans
Rated Thrust, each—	14,000 lbf (62.3 kN)
Thrust with Aftereburner, each—	23,100 lbf (102.7 kN)
Dimensions:	
Wing Span – Unswept:	64 ft 1.5in (19.5 m)
– Swept:	38 ft 2.5 in (5.5 m)
– Storage:	33 ft 3in (9.8 m)
Length:	62 ft 8 in (19.1 m)
Height:	32 ft 8.5 in (10.0 m)
Performance:	
Max level speed at altitude –	1,584 mph (2,550 km/h) (Mach 2.4)
Max speed at Sea Level—	913 mph (1,470 km/h) (Mach 1.2)
Cruising speed –	460 to 633 mph (740 to 1,020 km/h)
Service ceiling – Over	50,000 ft. (15,240 m)

Armament: One 20 mm Vulcan cannon; four AIM-7 Sparrow air-to-air missiles, or four AIM-54 Phoenix missiles attached to pallets on bottom of fuselage; two wing pylons capable of carrying a variety of missiles or bombs.

THIS AIRCRAFT IS ON LOAN FROM THE NATIONAL MUSEUM OF NAVAL AVIATION PENSACOLA, FLORIDA

The F-14 *Tomcat* is a supersonic, twin-engine, twin-tail, variable sweep wing, two-place fighter flown by the Navy as a carrier or land-based multirole fighter. It was the first of the fighters designed to incorporate air combat experience from Vietnam against Soviet Union MiG aircraft. It entered service in 1972 where it continued until replaced by the F/A-18 'Hornet' in 2006.

Grumman was selected to build the Navy's new carrier-based fighter in January 1969, with first flight of the F-14 *Tomcat* prototype taking place on December 21, 1970. Initial deployment with the fleet began in October 1972. Continued development and improvements of its capabilities made it an effective deterrent to any hostile threats to U.S. Navy carrier groups for over 30 years.

As the world's premier air defense fighter, it could simultaneously track up to 24 targets with its advanced weapons control system, while attacking six at once with *Phoenix* AIM-54A missiles. The *Tomcat* is well known for its prominent role in *"Top Gun"*, the 1986 movie about naval aviators. The success of the film spurred a video game franchise and a surge in U.S. Navy Flight Training recruiting.

The museum's Tomcat was initially assigned to VF-124, the F-14 Pacific Fleet crew training squadron. After two years as a trainer, our *Tomcat* went to the fleet for the remainder of its 14 years of operational service. Assignments included the famous VF-2 *'Bounty Hunters'*, while its final squadron was the *'Black Lions'* of VF-213, part of Carrier Air Wing Eight (CVW-8), assigned to the USS Theodore Roosevelt (CVN-71). Its final combat sortie was February 7, 2006. Following launch from the USS Roosevelt at 1600, *'Black Lion'* AJ-210 flew to Northern Iraq for overhead protection of U.S. and Iraq forces. After its mission, our *Tomcat* 'trapped' aboard its carrier at 2233 hours, completing a 6.5-hour mission.

Returning to the U.S. in March 2006, the F-14Ds were unloaded for the last time and retired. Our aircraft, BuNo 163897, was flown to McClellan shortly thereafter and joined the collection.

Museum Volunteers welcoming BuNo 163897 to McClellan, March 2006

MIKOYAN-GUREVICH MIG-17PF *FRESCO E*

SPECIFICATIONS:

Crew:	One Pilot
Power Plant:	One Klimov VK-1 turbojet
Thrust, w/afterburner —	5,955 lbf (26,500 newtons)
Dimensions:	
Span:	31 ft 7 in. (9.6 m)
Length:	40 ft. (12.2 m)
Height:	11 ft. (3.4 m)
Performance:	
Speed:	710 mph (1,143 km/h) at 10,000 ft., (Mach 0.975)
Ceiling:	57,000 ft. (17,373 m)
Range:	510 miles (820 km)

Armament:

Three 23 mm cannon in nose; provision for two under-wing packs of 8 x 55 mm air-to-air rockets or 1,100 lbs. (500 kg) of bombs.

THIS AIRCRAFT IS ON LOAN FROM THE NATIONAL MUSEUM OF THE USAF

The Mikoyan-Gurevich MiG-17PF was delivered as an all-weather interceptor version of the MiG-17. The design of the MiG-17 ensured improved high speed performance characteristics as a carry-over from its predecessor, the MiG-15. The prototype first flew on January 13, 1950. It was the first Soviet fighter to have an afterburning engine, the Klimov VK-1. The large wings with the large wing-fences allowed the Mig 17 to out turn most adversaries but the aircraft was limited in its rolling capabilities because it did not have hydraulic boosted control surfaces, as do fighters used by the United States.

The MiG-17PF featured the Izumrud radar, and three Nudelmann-Rikhter 23mm cannons. Over 9,000 of all versions of the MiG-17 were built in the Soviet Union, Poland, and China. A total of 104 MiG-17s were shot down by American fighters during the Vietnam War.

The museum's Fresco is a Polish built version, the PZL-Mielec Lim-5SP, built in 1959. It arrived by truck from Ellsworth AFB, South Dakota on October 12, 1993. How, when and where the USAF obtained it remains classified.

MIKOYAN-GUREVICH MIG-21F *FISHBED*

SPECIFICATIONS:

Crew:		One—pilot.
Power Plant:		One Tumansky afterburning turbojet. 14,000 lbf (62.3 kN)
Dimensions:		
Span:		27 ft. (8.2 m)
Length:		16 ft. (4.9 m)
Height:		16 ft. (4.9 m)
Weight:	Max Gross -	18,800 lbs. (8,526 kg)
Performance:		
Speed:		Mach 2.0
Ceiling:		56,000 ft. (17,070 m)
Combat radius:		375 miles (600 km)

Armament:

One 30 mm cannon in fuselage. Two "Atoll" air-to-air missiles under wing, or rocket pods with sixteen 57 mm rockets.

THIS AIRCRAFT IS ON LOAN FROM THE NATIONAL MUSEUM OF THE USAF

The Mikoyan-Gurevich MiG-21 first flew in 1956 as a short-range supersonic interceptor. Over 10,000 would be built in the years that followed. The aircraft has been used in combat by the Soviet Union, North Vietnam, India, Iraq, Egypt, and Syria. The USAF has flown several examples in fighter combat training, and others are now available to civilian owners, and may occasionally be seen at air shows. During the Vietnam War the MiG-21 was the most capable adversary for U. S. flyers who fought them in F-4 and F-105 fighters. There were 85 claimed shoot downs of Mig-21s in the Vietnam War.

The museum's aircraft is an S-107 (S/N 0201), which is the Czech built version of the MiG-21F-13, and was built at the Aero plant outside of Prague, Czechoslovakia. It was delivered to the Czech Air Force on June 5, 1966, and served until early 1989. It was purchased in Hungary by a U.S. citizen and shipped to the U.S. through Hamburg, West Germany. Along with S/N 0301, our S-107 was traded to the USAF Museum, with 0301 going to the main museum at Wright-Patterson AFB, Ohio. The Aerospace Museum of California's MiG-21 was reassembled in 15 hours, and became the first MiG-21 to go on permanent display in the U.S. when it entered the museum's Air Park on May 25, 1989.

SIKORSKY CH-3E
JOLLY GREEN GIANT

SPECIFICATIONS:

Accommodation:		Crew of three and up to 25 troops.
Dimensions:		
Rotor Diameter:		62 ft 0 in. (18.9 m)
Length:		73 ft 0 in. (22.25 m)
Height:		18 ft 1 in. (5.5 m)
Weight:	Empty—	12,423 lbs. (5,634 kg)
	Gross—	22,050 lbs. (10,000 kg)
Performance:		
Max. Speed:		164 mph (264 km/h)
Service Ceiling:		13,600 ft. (4,145 m)
Range:		480 miles (740 km)
Power Plants:		Two General Electric T58-GE-5 turboshaft engines 1,500 hp (1,119 kW) each

THIS AIRCRAFT IS ON LOAN FROM THE NATIONAL MUSEUM OF THE USAF

USAF interest in the S-61 Navy helicopter resulted in the purchase of the first three units for use in servicing radar sites in the Atlantic Ocean, often called "Texas Towers". These aircraft were designated as CH-3Bs. The fitting of the 1,500 hp T58-GE-5 engines for the original 1,300 hp units resulted in a re-designation of the craft to CH-3E. Versions equipped with armor-plate, refueling probe, and machine gun armament served with the Air-Sea Rescue units in Vietnam, where the aircraft was given the nickname "Jolly Green Giant".

USAF S/N 65-5690 was manufactured by Sikorsky Aircraft, Bridgeport, Connecticut, and was delivered to the Air Force on October 29, 1965. It was assigned to the 2nd Air Division (PACAF), Tan Son Nhut AFB, Vietnam in December 1965. It was transferred to the 377th Combat Support Group (PACAF), Tan Son Nhut AFB, in April, 1966; and the 20th Helicopter Squadron (PACAF), Tan Son Nhut, in October 1966; 14th AF Communications Wing (PACAF), Tan Son Nhut, in December 1966, and subsequently to Nha Trang AFB, Vietnam in July 1968, and 14th Special Operations Wing (PACAF), Udorn AFB, Thailand in August 1968. It was modified to CH-3E configuration and assigned to the 56th Special Operations Wing (PACAF), Udorn AFB. In August 1971 it was transferred to the 355th Tactical Fighter Wing (TAC), Davis-Monthan AFB, Arizona; to the 432nd Technical Operations Group (TAC), and to the Military Aircraft Storage Center (AFLC), Davis-Monthan AFB, Arizona in January 1979. It was withdrawn and sent to the AF Flight Testing Center (AFSC), Edwards AFB, California in October 1979; and finally to the 129th Aerospace Rescue and Recovery Group (ANG), Moffett NAS, California. It was flown to the 55th Air Rescue and Recovery Squadron (MAC), McClellan AFB, California, on September 25, 1990, and turned over to the museum for display.

PAISECKI CH-21C
WORKHORSE

SPECIFICATIONS:

Accommodation:		Crew of two pilots and up to 20 troops.
Dimensions:		
Rotor Diameter:		44 ft 6 in. (13.6 m)
Length:		86 ft 4 in. (26.3 m)
Height:		15 ft 5 in. (4.7 m)
Weight:	Empty:	8,000 lbs. (3,628 kg)
	Gross:	13,000 lbs. (5,896 kg)
Performance:		
Max. Speed:		131 mph (211 km/h)
Service Ceiling:		9,450 ft. (2,880 m)
Range:		265 miles (426 km)

Power Plant: One 1,425 hp (1,063 kW) Wright R-1820-103, 9-cylinder air-cooled engine

OWNED BY THE AEROSPACE MUSEUM OF CALIFORNIA

Based upon the earlier Navy HRP-2, the Piasecki (now Boeing Vertol) H-21 was the first tandem rotor helicopter to enter USAF service. It was used in both the air-rescue and troop carrier missions, and could carry either 20 troops or 12 litters. The H-21 first flew on April 11, 1952. The USAF "*Workhorse*" was also known as the "*Flying Banana*," and in U.S. Army service as the "*Shawnee*." It was the first helicopter to see service in the Vietnam War. The improved CH-21C featured an auto-pilot, provisions for external fuel tanks, and increased armor protection.

USAF S/N 51-15886 is a CH-21C-PH, one of 334 CH-21Cs built by Piasecki Helicopter in Morton, Pennsylvania. It was delivered to the USAF on September 10, 1954 and assigned to the 6510th Air Base Wing (ARDC), Edwards AFB, California. In January 1956 it was transferred to the U.S. Army. No records have been located for service with the Army.

CH-21C, S/N 51-15886 was purchased from the government as surplus property by a private individual residing in Williams, California, for $2,450 on August 19, 1970. He then sold it to Aviation Contractors Inc., of the same address, in November 1971.

Aviation Contractors, Inc. subsequently sold S/N 51-15886 to Lassen Air in June 1974, who registered it as N48082 and intended to use it for Agricultural Frost Control, i.e., as a wind machine to minimize crop damage due to frost, operating between the Chico area and Grass Valley, California. By April 1979 the airframe had a total of 849 hours of flight. Lassen Air later sold it to Aero Union, of Chico, California, in April 1986. Aero Union later restored the aircraft to static condition and delivered it to the museum, where it was placed on display December 20, 1989.

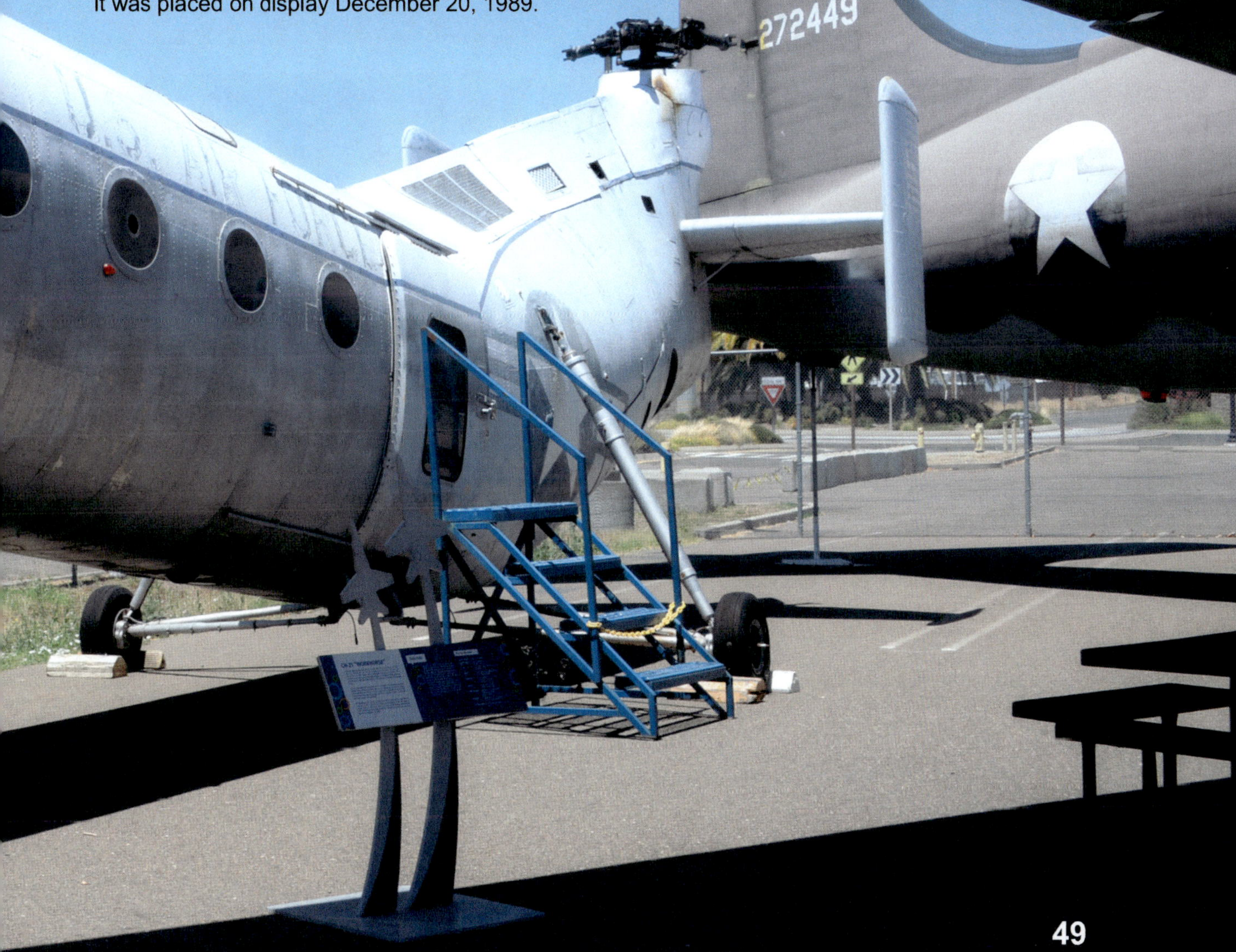

GYRODYNE QH-50D *DASH*

SPECIFICATIONS:

Crew:	None, Remotely Controlled
Power Plant:	One 365 hp Boeing T50-BO-12 turboshaft engine.
Dimensions:	
Rotor Diameter:	20 ft 0 in. (6.1 m)
Length:	5 ft 6.5 in. (1.7 m)
Height:	9 ft 8.5 in. (2.96 m)
Weight: Empty -	1,035 lbs. (470 kg)
Gross -	2,250 lbs. (1,020 kg)
Performance:	
Max. Speed:	88 mph (142 km/h)
Max Rate of Climb:	1,880 ft per minute, (573 m/min)
Service Ceiling:	16,000 ft.
Range:	80 miles. (130 km)
Payload:	2 Mk 44 homing torpedoes or 1 Mk 17 Nuclear depth charge

OWNED BY THE AEROSPACE MUSEUM OF CALIFORNIA

Development of the QH-50 Drone Anti-Submarine Helicopter (DASH) by the Long Island based *Gyrodyne Company of America* started in the late 1950s to counter the threat to U.S. Navy carriers by the growing number of Soviet submarines. DASH incorporated many technological innovations that enabled it to operate under the difficult conditions at sea. It was designed to be deployed on destroyers allowing each ship to cover a 60 mile diameter circle of ocean. The DASH's counter-rotating rotors powered by a turbine engine provided the lift and stability to carry two anti-submarine torpedoes or one nuclear depth charge slung between its landing skids.

The first operational model, the QH-50C, was deployed on the destroyer *USS Buck* (DD-761) in January 1963, but overall deployment to the U.S. fleet was delayed by vibration problems until July 1963. The D model entered the fleet in 1967. Crews were trained at either San

Counter-rotating rotors and control linkage

Front view: Screened air inlet to T50 turbine engine, side exhausts, and under slung torpedoes.

Clemente Island off San Diego or at FIS Dam Neck, Virginia. *Gyrodyne* provided technical support for the DASH system at naval bases around the continental Unites States as well as in Italy, the Philippines and Japan.

Production began with the XRON-1 (designation later changed to QH-50A) in 1960 and ended with the D model in 1969. A total of 784 were built. Of that number, 395 examples were the more capable QH-50D model seen here. The museum's QH-50D, SerNo DS-1660, served aboard the *USS Lowry* from April 1968 through June 1969. It was later assigned to the *USS Stormes* from November 1969 to September 1970 when it was transferred to Davis-Monthan AFB in Tucson, AZ before being used at the China Lake Naval Weapons test area from 1970 to 1971. Then after 15 years of storage it was transferred with 12 others to the U. S. Army in 1997 and served as a target tug at the White Sands Missile test Range until declared surplus in 2006. In 2009 it was obtained by the *Gyrodyne Helicopter Historical Foundation* and fully restored on behalf of the museum.

SOUNDING ROCKET-1950s/1980s

AEROJET
AEROBEE 350

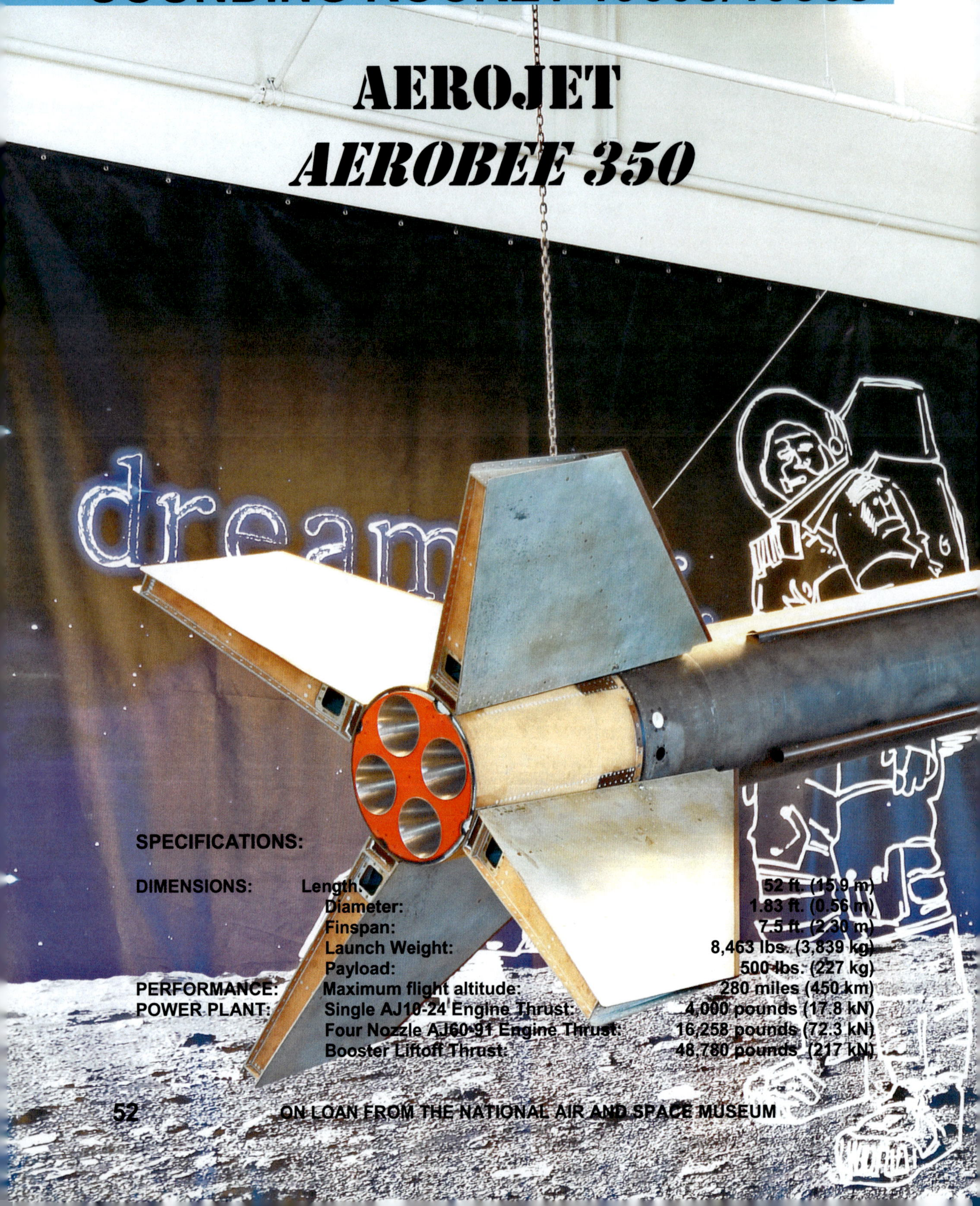

SPECIFICATIONS:

DIMENSIONS:	**Length:**	**52 ft. (15.9 m)**
	Diameter:	**1.83 ft. (0.56 m)**
	Finspan:	**7.5 ft. (2.30 m)**
	Launch Weight:	**8,463 lbs. (3,839 kg)**
	Payload:	**500 lbs. (227 kg)**
PERFORMANCE:	**Maximum flight altitude:**	**280 miles (450 km)**
POWER PLANT:	**Single AJ10-24 Engine Thrust:**	**4,000 pounds (17.8 kN)**
	Four Nozzle AJ60-91 Engine Thrust:	**16,258 pounds (72.3 kN)**
	Booster Liftoff Thrust:	**48,780 pounds (217 kN)**

ON LOAN FROM THE NATIONAL AIR AND SPACE MUSEUM

The *Aerobee* sounding rocket was an unguided suborbital sounding rocket for use in high altitude atmospheric and cosmic radiation research. It was initially sponsored by the US Navy. Recovery of payloads, and in some cases the entire vehicle, was by parachute. It was built by Aerojet General and first test fired in November 1947, reaching an altitude of 34.7 miles (55.8 km).

Research accomplishments made possible by the *Aerobee* included finding the Earth's protective radiation barrier, the Van Allen Radiation Belt. These sounding rockets were taking multi-spectral photos of far away star fields ten years before the first satellites.

There were nine major variants of the *Aerobee*, the *Aerobee 350* being the final version. In total 1,025 Aerobees were built, achieving 1,037 launches and a 97% reliability record. Launch sites were in New Mexico, Virginia, Manitoba, Canada, Woomera, Australia, and from the US Navy's research vessel, *USS Norton Sound*. The last Aerobee launch was on January 17, 1985.

The *Aerobee 350* (100 pound payload to 350 miles) was conceived in 1957, approved by NASA in 1961, and first flew in December, 1964. Maximum altitude achieved was 298 miles (480 km). Most *Aerobees* used a single Aerojet AJ10-24 liquid-fueled rocket engine using nitric acid/aniline fuel. For the *Aerobee 350* four of these engine nozzles were used and designated the AJ60-91, giving a significant increase in payload and performance. Twenty *Aerobee 350s* were launched, the last in May 1984.

The rocket on display is a NACA *Aerobee 350* model, Serial No. NASA-014, delivered in December 1967. It is displayed without its solid-fueled rocket booster.

SPACE ROCKET-1989/2018

AEROJET

DELTA II, SECOND STAGE

SPECIFICATIONS:

DIMENSIONS:	Length:	174.8 in. (4.44 m)
	Diameter:	68.7 in. (1.74 m)
	Fuel Tank Length:	109.5 in. (2.78 m)
	Weight at Launch:	14,354 lbs. (6,513 kg)
PERFORMANCE:	Payload:	771 lbs. (350 kg)
	Maximum Orbital Altitude:	19,320 miles (31,092km)
POWER PLANT:	AJ10-118 Engine Thrust:	9,850 lbs. (43.8 kN)
	Tank /Combustion Pressure:	221 psia/125 psig (1.52/0.86 MPa)
	Burn Time:	426 seconds (7.1 min)
	Fuel & Oxidizer Burned:	13,320 lbs. (6,044 kg)
	Specific Impulse:	314.2 seconds

OWNED BY AEROSPACE MUSEUM, DONATED BY AEROJET-ROCKETDYNE

This Delta II Second Stage was used on the very successful family of McDonnell Douglas Delta rockets that first launched February 14, 1989 and began a series of 155 launches, of which 153 were successful. The vehicle was used by NASA, USAF and commercial interests to place satellites in both low and geo stationary Earth orbits, as well as many science missions, including launching the Mars Rovers. The last mission was September 15, 2018.

Japan also used the Delta II Second Stage for launching some of their satellites, and the example on display is from that program. It was designed to place 350 kG in geo synchronous orbit at 19,320 nautical miles.

The engine is the Aerojet AJ10-118FJ, a development of the AJ10-24 used on many of the earlier Aerobee sounding rockets. The hypergolic (spontaneously combusts upon contact) fuel and oxidizer used was Aerozine-50 and Nitrogen Tetroxide (N_2O_4) respectively.

As configured, the second stage could be shutdown, and then restarted as needed for the specific mission.

The efficiency of a rocket engine is determined by the "expansion ratio" or "area ratio" of the rocket nozzle throat to exit. For the geo synchronous missions this was set at 65:1, resulting in an exit diameter of 68.7 inches (1.74 m) for the nozzle. As displayed the nozzle is only 47.5 inches in diameter, 38.2:1 expansion ratio, a consequence of this being an engine used for testing and it operated only at sea-level. Consequently the usual overall length of the second stage is 174.8 inches, where the mission units were 201.7 inches long (5.123 m).

RAVEN RX7 *RALLY* HOT AIR BALLOON

SPECIFICATIONS, RX7:

Accommodation:

Minimum Crew:	One (Pilot)
Maximum Occupants:	Not to exceed MTOM

Power Plant: Single Burner with two Propane bottles

Dimensions:

Envelope Diameter:	55 ft. (16.76 m)
Envelope Height:	55 ft. (16.7 m)
Envelope Volume:	77,500 cu ft. (2,196 cu m)
Envelope Weight:	205 lbs (93 kg)
Empty Weight, Basket, Burner, Envelope:	approx 465 pounds (210 kg)
Weight: Maximum Take-Off Mass (MTOM)	1,480 lbs (662 kg)

Performance:

Envelope Temperature, Not to Exceed:	250 degF (120 degC)
Maximum Wind at Takeoff:	15 knots (7.7 m/sec)
Maximum Surface Wind with Passengers:	10 knots (5.1 m/sec)
Maximum Rate of Climb:	1,000 ft/min (5 m/sec)
Nominal Lift at Sea Level:	75 degF (24 degC): 1,163 lb (527 kg)
Nominal Lift at Sea Level:	75 degF (24 degC): 15 lb/1,000 cubic feet

OWNED BY AEROSPACE MUSEUM OF CALIFORNIA

Man first flew under crude hot air balloons in 1783 over France. Ballooning has continued to be a preferred way for tranquil flight and a bird's eye view of the world below. Its popularity continues and the Raven RX7 is an example of the modern balloon. Flight is achieved due to the difference between the weights of the warmed air (less dense) within the balloon enclosure compared to the weight of the displaced cooler ambient air.

The RX7 Rally manned Hot Air Balloons were manufactured by Raven/Aerostar Inc., in Sioux Falls, South Dakota. They are certificated for Airworthiness by the FAA and described in Type Certificate A15CE. Examples are flown in both the USA and Europe.

The RX7 manned Hot Air Balloon basket and burner are used with a 77,500 cubic foot balloon envelope (2,200 cubic meters), which is 55 feet (16.76 meters) in diameter. The RX7 was introduced in the late 1970s and over 3,000 examples were built. Production ended in 2007. Balloon envelopes are typically constructed with twenty-four horizontally cut, bulbous gores of ripstop nylon fabric (parachute cloth), coated to make it airtight and to protect it from the effects of sunlight. Envelopes are typically of the 'inverted teardrop' shape.

Only the woven wicker basket, burner and skirt are displayed, as the entire hot air envelope is far too large for indoor display. The displayed vehicle is Model RX-7, S/N RX7-331, which flew as N4099V.

Balloon basket and skirt donated by Bryon Stevenson.

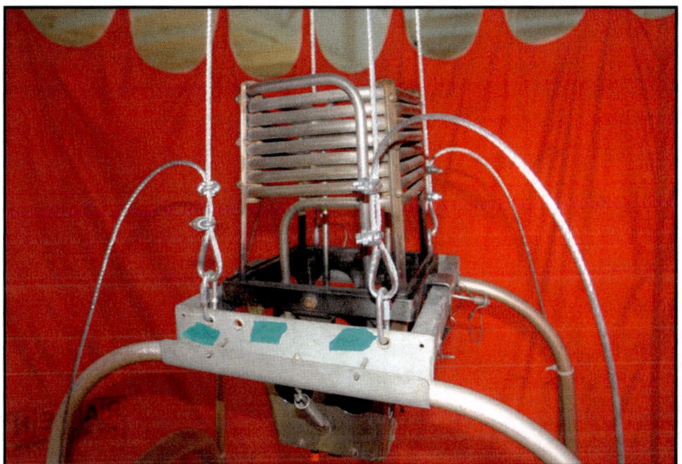

Overhead Balloon propane burner and gasifier. The tubing coiled around the burner flame preheats the propane and insures it is a gas when injected into the burner.

The balloon propane burner is seen just over the pilot's head. He pulls a lanyard to control the amount of flame. The resulting heated air causes the balloon to rise, when the air cools it descends. Periodically firing the burner maintains the desired altitude.

RUTAN MODEL 54
QUICKIE

SPECIFICATIONS:

Crew:	**One, pilot**
Powerplant:	**1× Onan 2-cylinder, converted generator engine, 22 hp at 3,800 rpm**
Dimensions:	
Length:	**19 ft 10 in (6.0 m)**
Wingspan:	**16 ft 8 in (5.1 m)**
Height:	**4 ft 5 in (1.34 m)**
Wing area:	**67 ft² (6.2 m²)**
Empty weight:	**290 lb (132 kg)**
Max takeoff weight:	**800 lb (363 kg)**
Performance:	
Maximum speed:	**180 mph (290 km/h)**
Cruise speed:	**140 mph (225 km/h)**
Range:	**550 mi (885 km)**
Rate of climb:	**900 ft/min (275 m/min)**
Ceiling:	**9,500 ft (2,900 m)**

OWNED BY THE AEROSPACE MUSEUM OF CALIFORNIA

The *Quickie* is a lightweight, single seat, homebuilt aircraft designed by Burt Rutan. One of the dozens of unconventional aircraft created for the general aviation market, the *Quickie* is Model 54 in Rutan's design series. It is a tandem wing aircraft; both the front and rear wings are full airfoils. The forward wing is technically a canard, fitted with elevators, but it provides about 60% of the lift. The aft wing serves as horizontal tail, although all pitch control comes from the forward canard. Highly efficient, and of composite construction, the *Quickie* is typical of Rutan's aircraft designs.

Construction of the prototype commenced in August of 1977 at the Scaled Composites facility in Mojave, California. The design was frozen in January 1978. It was optimized to consist of a minimal number of fiberglass components, with the fuselage, front wing and rear wing forming a single unit, and the empennage, with vertical tail, comprising the other. Integration of components and ease of construction were given high priorities during the design phase. The choice of engines that could be fitted to the aircraft was very wide, but for simplicity the prototype used a VW Beetle flat-four engine.

Rutan later stated that the design was meant to echo the design of X-Wing fighter from the hit film *Star Wars*, which debuted in 1977. The *Quickie* was an attractive and exciting aircraft for a first-time kit aircraft builder. Kit production commenced in June 1978 and by the late 1990s over 3,000 single and two seater kits had been produced and sold.

Aircraft donated to AMC by John Macomas via Bill Mauser. Painted by Kracon Aircraft of Lincoln, California

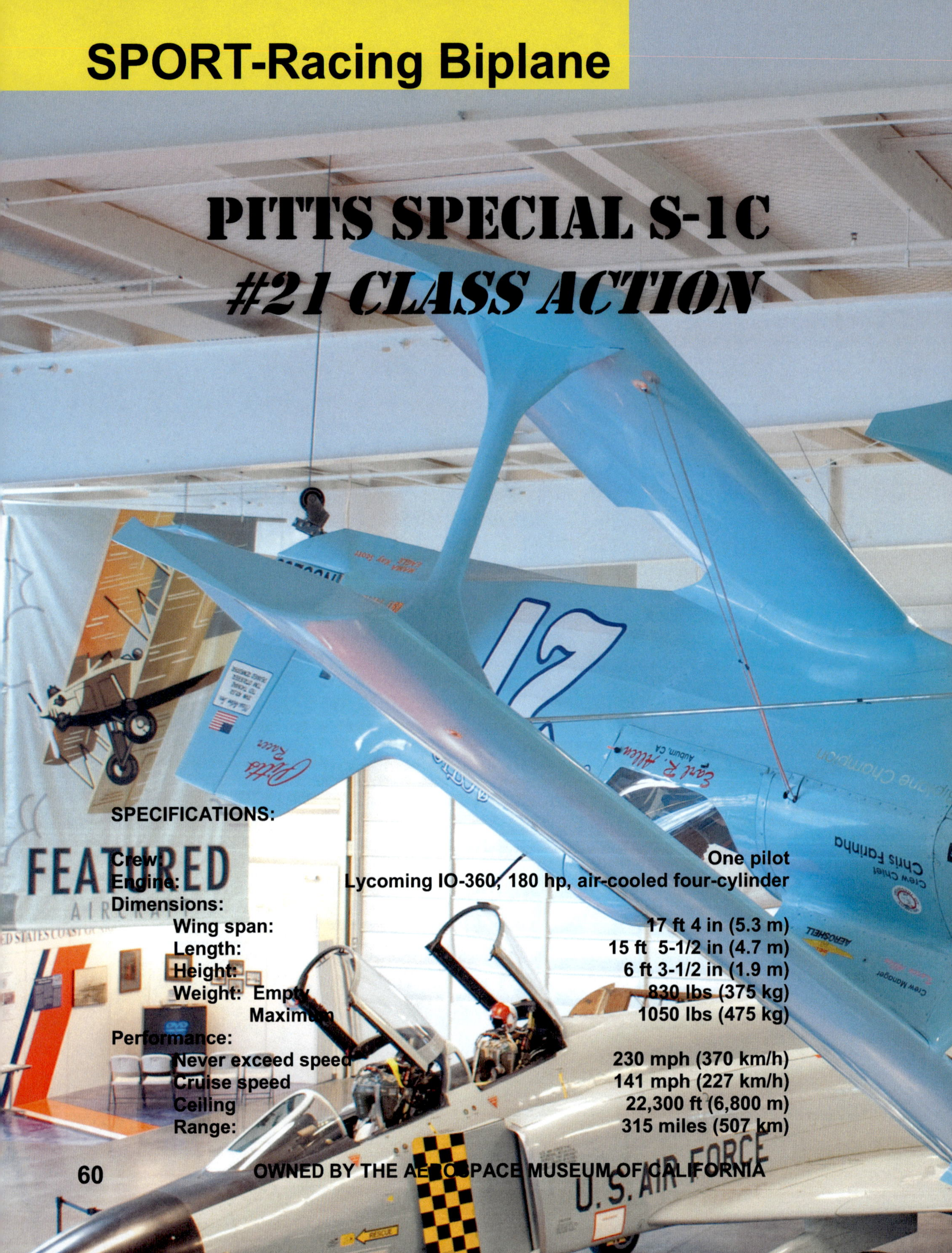

PITTS SPECIAL S-1C
#21 CLASS ACTION

SPECIFICATIONS:

Crew:	**One pilot**
Engine:	**Lycoming IO-360, 180 hp, air-cooled four-cylinder**
Dimensions:	
Wing span:	**17 ft 4 in (5.3 m)**
Length:	**15 ft 5-1/2 in (4.7 m)**
Height:	**6 ft 3-1/2 in (1.9 m)**
Weight: Empty	**830 lbs (375 kg)**
Maximum	**1050 lbs (475 kg)**
Performance:	
Never exceed speed	**230 mph (370 km/h)**
Cruise speed	**141 mph (227 km/h)**
Ceiling	**22,300 ft (6,800 m)**
Range:	**315 miles (507 km)**

OWNED BY THE AEROSPACE MUSEUM OF CALIFORNIA

In 1943, Curtis Pitts decided to build himself an aerobatic airplane. "I only intended to build one airplane – for myself", he later admitted. But despite his intentions, the airplane caught on. Requests for plans soon came in so he and his son formed a company, Pitts Aviation Enterprises, to provide them to homebuilders. One of the most successful examples was the "Little Stinker", made for Miss Betty Skelton, an internationally known aerobatic display pilot. In 1977 the manufacturing rights and sales were sold to a new company, which was named Pitts Aerobatics.

Our S-1C *Pitts Special* was built by Donald L. Merriman from plans by Curtis Pitts, the designer, and sold to Tom Wrolstad of Molalla, OR. It was completed on July 7, 1973. A single place, acrobatic bi-plane, it would be used as a racer until its last race in 1997.

Racing procedure is to have all aircraft within a class qualify. The fastest six participate in the Gold race, and the second fastest group in the Silver. The winner of the Silver gets to participate in the Gold. First raced at Merced, CA, June 1, 1974, it finished 3rd place in the Gold race. In subsequent races that year it placed 4th in the Gold at Mohave, was 1st place in the Silver and was Champion at Reno that year.

The aircraft sat idle from 1975 thru 1987. That year it placed 3rd in the Gold at Reno. In 1988 it placed 5th. In 1989 it was sold to Legal Eagle Racing of Birmingham, AL. From 1989 thru 1997, the aircraft placed 2nd six times in Gold races, 3rd in one; and was 1st and Champion in '94 and '97, the last year it flew in competition.

The aircraft sat idle in storage until 2006 when it was restored by the owners, John Adler, Tom Strueber and Deanes Rowedder, then donated to the Museum.

PROBER
PIXIE N7035M

SPECIFICATIONS:

CREW:		One (pilot)
DIMENSIONS:	Wing Span:	29 ft., 10 in. (9.09 m)
	Length:	17 ft., 3 in. (5.26 m)
	Height:	6 ft., 2 in. (1.88 m)
	Empty Weight:	543 lbs. (246 kg)
	Gross Weight:	900 lbs. (408 kg)
PERFORMANCE:	Max. Speed:	130 mph (209 km/h)
	Cruising Speed:	83 mph (135 km/h)
	Range:	290 miles (467 km)
	Service Ceiling:	12,500 ft. (3,810 m)
POWER PLANT:		Converted Volkswagen Engine Continental A-65 or Limbach SL 1700 EA – 60 hp (44.7 kW)

ON LOAN FROM THE ROBERT GILBERT FAMILY

The Pober *Pixie* is a single-seat, open cockpit, parasol-winged monoplane equipped with fixed landing gear, tail wheel and initially powered by a converted Volkswagen engine. In response to the 1973 oil crisis, the Experimental Aircraft Association (EAA) launched "Project Econoplane" to develop an aircraft with high fuel economy that would be affordable for its members to build and operate. The Paul Poberenzny designed *Pober Pixie*, loosely derived from the 1930s Heath *Parasol* (the first successful "kit" airplane) was the result, with fuel consumption of 3 to 3.5 U.S. gallons per hour. Plans were completed in January 1974 and the prototype flew in late July, in time for the EAA Annual Convention that year. After the EAA convention the prototype was equipped with the Limbach SL 1700 EA engine (60 hp @ 3550 rpm) and Rehm 53-30 two-blade fixed-pitch propeller, which became the standard set-up for production kits.

The *Pixie* fuselage is fabricated from welded 4130 steel tube, while the wings are made from Sitka spruce covered with Stits Poly-fiber fabric.

The Pober *Pixie* is easy to fly and economical to run. It is roomy enough for larger pilots and has a cruise speed high enough for reasonable cross country trips. In many ways, the Pixie typified sport aviation, open cockpit flying: the helmet and goggle era that will never leave the aviation scene. It was the answer to many needs – not the least of which was economy.

N7035M began flying in Chico, California, in September 1993, powered by a Volkswagen Model 1600, 1835 cc, 60 horsepower engine. In 1997 it was sold to John Blotz of Oroville, CA, who in turn sold it to Rober Gilbert of Berry Creek, CA in March 2007. The Robert Gilbert family has loaned the aircraft to the museum.

PEREIRA GP-3
OSPREY 2 AMPHIBIAN

SPECIFICATIONS:

Crew: One pilot, and one passenger
Engine: Lycoming O-320-A2B; 150 hp (112 kW), air-cooled four-cylinder
Dimensions:
- Wing span: 26 ft 0 in (7.92 m)
- Wing Area: 130 sq. ft. ((12.08 sq m)
- Length: 20 ft 6 in (6.25 m)
- Height: 6 ft 0 in (1.83 m)
- Weight: Empty – 970 lbs (440 kg), Maximum – 1,560 lb (707 kg)

Performance:
- Cruise speed: 130 mph (209 km/h)
- Rate of Climb : 1,000 ft/min (5.1 m/s)
- Range: 500 miles (800 km)

OWNED BY AEROSPACE MUSEUM, DONATED BY JAMES BEHEL

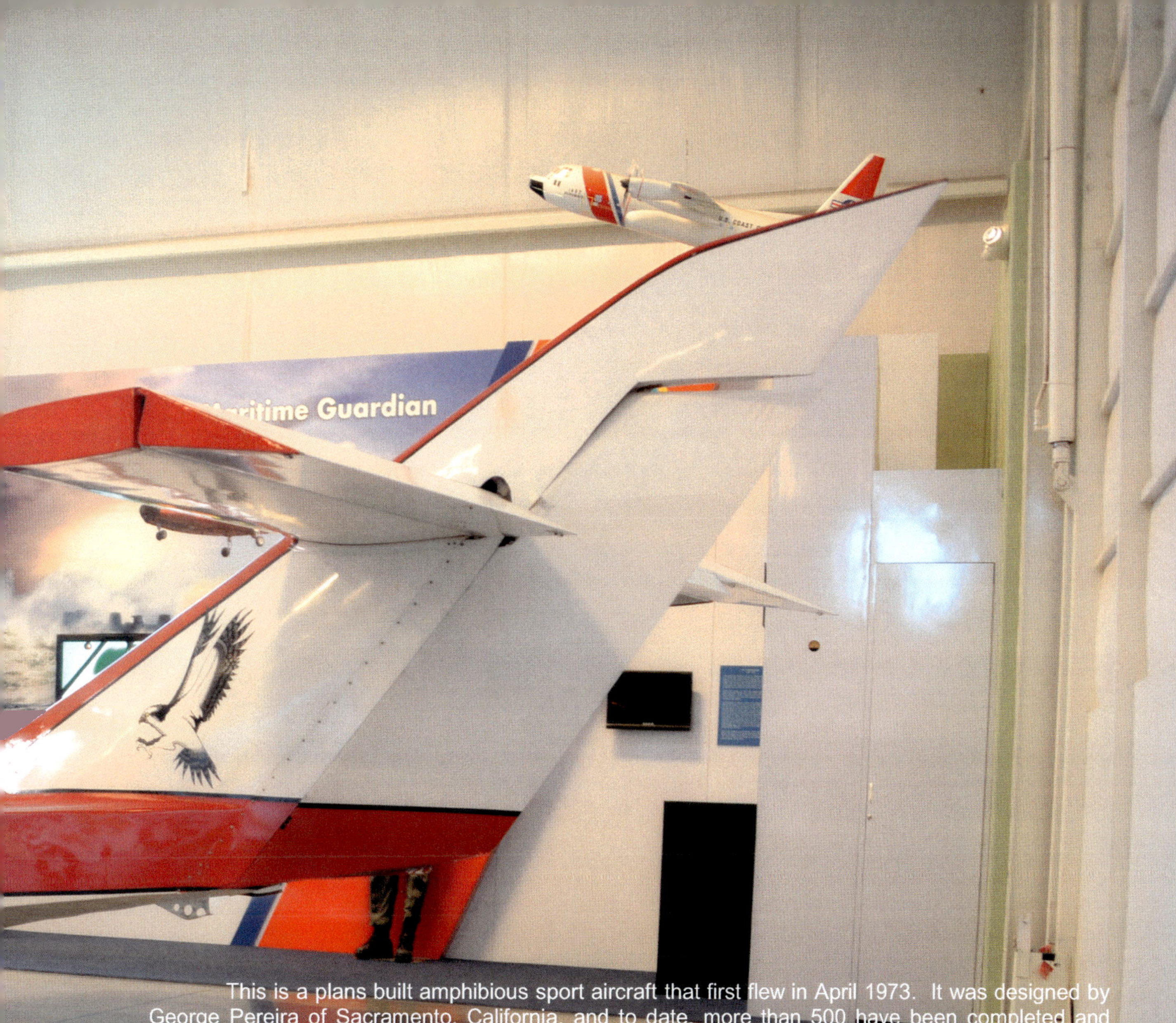

This is a plans built amphibious sport aircraft that first flew in April 1973. It was designed by George Pereira of Sacramento, California, and to date, more than 500 have been completed and flown. It is able to operate from both dry land, and water.

It is a mid-wing cantilever monoplane with a flying boat hull, its single engine is mounted as a pusher on struts in a nacelle above the fuselage. Side-by-side seating fully encloses both the pilot and passenger. Retractable tricycle undercarriage is used for land operations, with the main wheels folding into the undersides of the wings. Construction throughout is of wood; including the stressed skin, which is of thin plywood. Some of the hull contours are formed using polyurethane foam covered in fiberglass.

Amateur builders are able to construct the aircraft in as little as 16 ft x 26 ft (4.9 m x 7.9 m) of floor space, and requires 1,300 hours to complete.

PEREIRA GP-4 *HIGH PERFORMANCE OSPREY*

SPECIFICATIONS:

Crew:	One pilot, and one passenger
Engine:	Lycoming IO-360-A1A; 200 hp (149 kW), air-cooled four-cylinder
Dimensions:	
Wing span:	24 ft 0 in (7.3 m)
Length:	21 ft 6 in (6.55 m)
Wing Area:	104 sq ft (9.7 m^2)
Weight:	Empty – 1,260 lbs (572 kg), Maximum – 2,040 lb (925 kg)
Performance:	
Cruise Speed:	240 mph (386 km/h)
Never Exceed Speed:	255 mph (410 km/h)
Rate of Climb:	2,200 ft/min (11 m/s)
Service Ceiling:	20,000 ft (6,100 m)
Range:	1,100 miles (1,770 km)

OWNED BY AEROSPACE MUSEUM, DONATED BY JAMES BEHEL

The Osprey GP-4 is a homebuilt, experimental, aircraft available as either a kit or plans built. In 1984 the GP-4 won the Grand Champion Custom Built and the Outstanding New Design awards at the prestigious Experimental Aircraft Association Airventure airshow in Oshkosh, Wisconsin. It was the fourth aircraft designed by George Pereira of Sacramento, California.

The GP-4 is a high performance low-wing cantilever monoplane featuring side-by-side seating, retractable landing gear, and all wood construction. It has a single spar wing stressed +8 G and -6 G loading. The aircraft's wooden construction is labor-intensive, with an estimated 3,000-4,000 hours required to construct it.

The displayed aircraft, N59GP, was the prototype, Serial Number 1, completed 7/9/1984. It was subsequently donated to the Aerospace Museum by James Behel.

BELLMORE
FLIGHTSTAR II SL

SPECIFICATIONS:

CREW:		Two - side by side with dual controls
DIMENSIONS:	Wing Span:	32 feet (9.75 m)
	Length:	19 feet 7 inches (5.97 m)
	Height:	7 feet 10 inches (5.18 m)
	Empty Weight:	385 lbs. (175 kg)
	Maximum Take-off Weight:	950 lbs. (430 kg)
PERFORMANCE:	Maximum Speed:	96 mph (155 km/h)
	Cruise Speed:	65 mph (105 km/h)
	Climb Rate:	600 ft per minute (183 m/min)
	Maximum Range:	200 miles (322 km)

POWERPLANT OPTIONS:

50 hp (37.3 kW) Rotax 503, 2-cylinder, 2-cycle
64 hp (47.7 kW) Rotax 582, 2-cylinder, 2-cycle
or 60 hp (44.7 kW) HKS700E, 2-cylinder, 4-cycle

OWNED BY AEROSPACE MUSEUM OF CALIFORNIA

Flightstar is a large family of single and two-seat, high wing, single engine kit (homebuilt) aircraft designed by Tom Peghiny and produced by Flightstar Sportplanes of South Woodstock, Connecticut. The *Flightstar* is an ultra-light aircraft with a conventional three axis controls and the engine located in front of and above the cabin. The foldable wings have full-span ailerons, while the tail features conventional stabilizers with elevators and rudder. The first *Flightstar* was built around 1986. The early models qualify for the "Ultralight Vehicle" category (max empty weight 254 lbs) established by the Federal Aviation Administration.

The display aircraft is the heavier *Flightstar II SL* first flown in 1994 and designed as an improved "Sport Light" version with a canopy to serve as a trainer for any of the other *Flightstar* ultralight models. It is powered by the 64 hp Rotax 582, 2-cycle engine and was purchased and built by Jerome Bellmore of Wilton, California.

180 *Flightstar II SLs* were manufactured. In 2009, the company closed operations and the Flightstar line was sold to Yuneec International of China.

The aircraft was donated to the AMC by Jerry Bellmore.

FAIRCHILD PT-19B
CORNELL

SPECIFICATIONS: PT-19A/B and PT-26

Crew: Pupil and instructor in tandem cockpits.

Power Plant: One 175 h.p. Ranger L-440-1 inverted six-cylinder in-line, air-cooled engine

Dimensions:

Span –	36 ft 0 in (11.0 m)
Length –	28 ft 0 in (8.5 m)
Height –	10 ft 6 in (3.2 m)
Weights: Empty –	1,845 lb. (837 kg)
Gross –	2,545 lb (1,154 kg)

Performance:

Max. Speed –	132 mph (212 km/h)
Climb –	17.5 min to 10,000 ft. (3,050 m)
Service Ceiling –	15,300 ft (4,660 m)
Range –	400 statue miles, (644 km)

OWNED BY AEROSPACE MUSEUM OF CALIFORNIA

Although the peacetime Army Air Corps preferred bi-planes as primary trainers, a number of monoplanes were also pressed into service. The Fairchild M-62 was selected and ordered in large numbers to support the expanding Aviation Cadet program. Initially designated the PT-19, it would also be manufactured as the PT-23 with a radial engine in place of the air-cooled in-line Ranger engine.

The PT-26 would be the final version of the aircraft, similar to the PT–19 except for a full canopy, which covered both seats rather than previous open cockpits. This version was initially intended for the Royal Canadian Air Force pilot training program, but also saw service with the Army Air Corps. The PT-19B seen at the museum also has the full canopy.

This aircraft was stationed at Jones Field, Texas for its entire service career, and is painted as typical for the station. It was picked up as 'salvage' after lying unattended at Beale AFB, CA in 1988. Restoration efforts were initiated that year and then dropped due to the very poor condition of the aircraft and lack of parts. A crew of museum volunteers, reinitiated restoration in 2001, the completed aircraft went on display in 2009. This has entailed the fabrication of many parts to replace those that were missing or lost, and much tedious labor to bring the airframe and engine up to aircraft standards. Several team members provided financial sponsorship for the restoration supported by a lead gift provided in memory of Mr. & Mrs. Pinkney.

Upon completion, a portion of the airframe was covered in Plexiglas so that visitors can view construction details.

NORTH AMERICAN T-6G *TEXAN*

SPECIFICATIONS:

Crew:	Pilot & Passenger
Power Plant:	One Pratt & Whitney R-1340 radial, rated at 600 hp (447 kW)
Dimensions:	
Span:	42 ft 0 in (12.8 m)
Length:	29 ft (8.8 m)
Height:	11 ft 9 in (3.6 m)
Performance:	
Max. Speed:	205 mph (330 km/h) at 5,000 ft (1525 m)
Service Ceiling:	21,500 ft (6,553 m)
Range:	750 miles (1,207 km)

Armament: (W.W. II) One .30 caliber m/g on cowling; one .30 cal. m/g in right wing panel; provisions for one flexible .30 cal. m/g in rear cockpit.

THIS AIRCRAFT IS ON LOAN FROM THE NATIONAL MUSEUM OF THE USAF

The North American "Texan" began service as the AT-6, an advanced trainer during WWII, and served with the USAAF, USN, and Royal Canadian Air Forces where it was known as the "Harvard". Introduced in 1938, a total of 15,495 Texans were built during the war years, with 10,057 AT-6s going to the USAAF. In 1948 the aircraft was designated by the USAF as the T-6, where it was serving as the primary trainer for aviation students. During the Korean War, the aircraft saw service as a Forward Air Controller (FAC) craft, carrying smoke-rockets under the wing for marking targets for fighter-bombers. After the WWII many of the aircraft were overhauled and upgraded to the T-6G configuration, which included updated avionics, and a new canopy that provided better visibility. The T-6 remained in USAF service until 1955.

T-6G S/N 51-15124 was remanufactured and delivered with its new serial number to the Air Force on October 9, 1952 at the North American Aviation plant, Columbus, Ohio. It was assigned to the 3545th Pilot Training Wing (ATC), Goodfellow AFB, Texas on October 10, 1952. On January 24, 1953 it was transferred to the 3310th Tac Training Wing, Scott AFB, Illinois, where it remained until October 23, 1953 when it was transferred to Davis Monthan AFB, Arizona. For a brief period it was assigned to the Mobile Air Material Area, (AMC), Brookley AFB, Alabama, before being returned to Davis Monthan in December 1954. There is no subsequent history of the aircraft in USAF records. The aircraft was acquired at a later date, along with several others, from which several T-6 aircraft were made airworthy. 51-15124 contributed its serviceable components and became a display aircraft made up of components from several unairworthy aircraft. Although complete, it is not restored to flyable condition. It was placed on display in May 1994.

Liz Payne Photo

NORTH AMERICAN T-28B *TROJAN*

SPECIFICATIONS:

Crew:	Pilot & Passenger
Power Plant: T-28A	Wright R-1300-1 radial engine, 800 hp (597 kW)
T-28B	Lycoming built R-1820-86B radial, 1,425 hp (1,163 kW)
Dimensions:	
Span:	41 ft 1 in (12.5 m)
Length:	32 ft 0 in (9.75 m)
Height:	12 ft 8 in (3.9 m)
Weight: Empty -	5,111 lbs (2,318 kg)
Maximum Gross -	6,365 lbs (2,900 kg)
Performance:	
Max Speed: T-28A -	283 mph (455 km/h) at 5,900 ft (1,800 m)
T-28B -	346 mph (557 km/h)
Service Ceiling: T-28A-	29,000 ft (8,840 m)
T-28B-	37,000 ft (12,275 m)
Range: T-28A-	1,008 miles (1,622 km)
T-28B-	1,060 miles (1,706 km)

THIS AIRCRAFT IS ON LOAN FROM THE NATIONAL MUSEUM OF THE USAF

Built by North American as a replacement for the WWII T-6 *"Texan"*, it was adopted as a standard trainer for both the USAF and Navy in the 1950s. The T-28A was first delivered to the USAF in 1950 as a primary trainer. It was found unsatisfactory for the mission and was then used as a basic trainer until replaced by the Cessna T-37. The Navy T-28B and T-28C tailhook versions had a larger engine than the USAF model, and gave better performance, resulting in a very satisfactory aircraft. This R-1820 engine is an evolution of the engine that powered the Boeing B-17 heavy bomber of WW2.

Between 1962 and 1968, a number of T-28As were re-engined and modified to T-28D configuration as fighter-bombers to be supplied through the military Assistance Program to foreign nations, including South Vietnam and Cambodia.

The Museum's T-28B is U.S. Navy BuNo 138327 one of 489 T-28s built by North American Aviation at Columbus, Ohio. It was delivered to the Navy on September 22, 1955 to serve at NAS Pensacola, Florida. Its final USN assignment ended with VU-8 at Litchfield Park, Arizona on July 10, 1962. The U.S. Army Aviation Engineering Flight Test Activity at Edwards AFB, California then obtained it for their use on the Cheyenne helicopter test program. On March 27, 1987 this aircraft made the last flight of any U.S. military T-28 when it was flown to the museum from Edwards AFB.

LOCKHEED T-33A *SHOOTING STAR* *(T-BIRD)*

SPECIFICATIONS:

Crew:	**Two seats but only one pilot required.**
Power Plant:	**Allison J33-A-35 turbojet, thrust 5,400 lbf (24.0 kN)**
Dimensions:	
Span:	**38 ft 10-1/2 in (11.08 m)**
Length:	**37 ft 9 in (11.5 m)**
Height:	**11 ft 4 in (3.5 m)**
Weight: Empty-	**8,084 lbs (3,666 kg)**
Max Gross-	**11,965 lbs (5,426 kg)**
Performance:	
Max. Speed:	**534 mph (860 km/h) at 25,000 ft (7,620 m)**
Range:	**800 miles (1.290 km)**
Service Ceiling:	**45,500 ft (13,870 m)**
Armament:	**Two .50 cal. m/g in nose.**

THIS AIRCRAFT IS ON LOAN FROM THE NATIONAL MUSEUM OF THE USAF

Built by Lockheed Aircraft, this was the first jet trainer, a derivative of the original P-80 *"Shooting Star"*. It was needed to assist pilots in transitioning from propeller airplanes to the first jets, and featured a 38.6 inch addition in fuselage forward of the wing, and a 12 inch addition aft to provide room for the second seat. A 230 gallon fuel tank was added to each wing tip, and armament was reduced to two .50 caliber machine guns. First produced in 1948 as the TF-80C, it remained in operational service with the USAF until 1988, serving as a trainer and utility aircraft. In total, 6,557 were built, with license production also occurring in Canada and Japan. Some T-33As, supplied under the Military Assistance Program, are still in service today. T-33s were the primary trainer for undergraduate pilots in the advanced phase. In 1960-1980 the aircraft performed as target, as electronic counter measures platforms and other general support, including radar/radio verification, and cost-effective pilot proficiency training.

USAF S/N 53-5205 is a T-33A-1-LO, one of 5,691 T-33As built by Lockheed Aircraft in Burbank, California. It was delivered to the USAF on October 6, 1954 and assigned to the 2589th AF Reserve Combat Training Center, Dobbins AFB, Georgia. In May 1955 it went to the 2584th AFR Flying Training Center, Memphis Municipal Airport, Tennessee, and in October 1957 to the 1001st Air Base Wing Andrews AFB, Maryland. It was retired to Davis-Monthan AFB, Arizona in August 1962, and shipped to the museum in May 1983. It bears the insignia of its last assignment at Andrews AFB.

NORTH AMERICAN T-39A *SABRELINER*

SPECIFICATIONS:

Accommodations:	Two pilots and four passengers.
Power Plants:	Two Pratt & Whitney J60-P-3 turbojets, 3,000 lbf (13,345 newtons)
Dimensions:	
Span:	44 ft 5 in (13.5 m)
Length:	43 ft 9 in (13.3 m)
Height:	16 ft 0 in (4.9 m)
Weight: Empty -	9,300 lbs (4,218 kg)
Maximum Gross -	17,760 lbs (5,413 kg)
Performance:	
Max. Speed:	595 mph (958 km/h) at 36,000 ft (10,970 m)
Service Ceiling:	39,000 ft (10,970 m)
Range:	1,725 miles (2,775 km)

THIS AIRCRAFT IS ON LOAN FROM THE NATIONAL MUSEUM OF THE USAF

North American Aviation Corporation developed the *Sabreliner* as a private venture to meet a USAF requirement for a twin jet utility trainer. The prototype T-39 made its first flight on September 16, 1958, followed by the first flight of the T-39A on June 30, 1960. The USAF and USN purchased a total of 211. They used it as a utility transport, small cargo flights, and for pilot proficiency training. After military production commitments were met North American offered it on the commercial market as the *Sabreliner*. There it became the first successful business jet. The USAF changed the designation to CT-39A in June 1977. It carried a crew of two, with room for four passengers.

USAF S/N 61-660 is a T-39A-1-NA, one of 143 T-39As built for the USAF by North American Aviation in Inglewood, California. It was delivered to the USAF in June 1962 and assigned to the 3902nd Air Base Wing (SAC), Offutt AFB, Nebraska. In April 1963 it was sent to the 22nd Bomb Wing (SAC), March AFB, California. In January 1974 it went to the 6th Bomb Wing (SAC), Minot AFB, North Dakota, then returned to the 22nd Bomb Wing in February 1974. From June 1975 it was assigned to either the 1400th Military Airlift Squadron (MAC), McClellan AFB, California; or the 63rd Military Airlift Wing (MAC), Norton AFB, California. It was retired to the museum in August 1985.

HUNTING/BAC
JET PROVOST T MK 3A

SPECIFICATIONS:

CREW:		Two pilots – side by side
DIMENSIONS:	Wing Span:	35 ft., 4 in. (10.77 m)
	Length:	34 ft., 0 in. (10.36 m)
	Height:	10 ft., 2 in. (3.10 m)
	Empty Weight:	4,888 lbs. (2,217 kg)
	Gross Weight:	6,989 lbs. (3,170 kg)
PERFORMANCE:	Max. Speed:	440 mph (708 km/h)
	Service Ceiling:	36,750 ft. (11,200 m)
	Range:	900 mi. (1,448 km)
POWER PLANT:		1 Armstrong Siddeley Viper 102 turbojet
	Takeoff Thrust:	1750 lbs. (7.8 kN)

THIS AIRCRAFT IS ON LOAN FROM JON R. TODD AND KEN McDERMOTT

In the early 1950's, the Royal Air Force (RAF) sought a new jet training aircraft. Hunting developed the Jet Provost Trainer Mark I from the Hunting-Percival piston engined Provost basic trainer to meet the requirement. Delivery of forty Mark T Mk 3s began in 1959. These differed from the first 16 airplanes as they were fitted with the more powerful Armstrong Siddeley Viper 5 jet engine, Martin-Baker ejection seats, a re-designed canopy, wing-tip fuel tanks and shortened landing gear struts.

The Jet Provost was used as a trainer aircraft, military flying team display aircraft and later for air warfare and tactical weapons training. Hunting became a part of the British Aircraft Corp. (BAC) in 1959, going on to build a total of 741 Jet Provost aircraft, 201 as T Mk 3s, a number of which were sold to foreign countries. In addition, BAC developed the *Strikemaster* ground attack version, which is also used by a number of foreign air forces, a total of 146 being built.

Jet Provost T Mk 3A, XN472, was delivered to the RAF in 1960 and was upgraded to T Mk 3A standard in January 1974 and operated as No. 86. In March 1988 it was transferred to No. 2 School of Technical Training at Cosford for ground instructional use and designated 8959M/J. On November 1993 it was tendered and sold to Global Aviation and exported to the US. It appears in FAA records in March 1995 when sold to an aircraft company in Denver, Colorado. It was next sold to Jon Todd, of Georgetown, California in January 1997, registered as N3497N. The aircraft was re-registered as N69RT and coded 69. In 1999 a second owner, Kenneth McDermott, was taken on. The aircraft is painted in the colors of a RAF training aircraft.

BEECH UC-45J
EXPEDITER

SPECIFICATIONS:

Crew:	Two, six to eight passengers.
Power Plants:	Two Pratt & Whitney, Wasp Junior, R-985-AN-3 engines.
Dimensions:	
Span:	47 ft 8 in (14.5 m)
Length:	34 ft 3 in (10.4 m)
Height:	9 ft 8 in (2.9 m)
Weight: Empty-	5,890 lbs (2, 670 kg)
Maximum Gross-	7,850 lbs (3,560 kg)
Performance:	
Max. Speed:	215 mph (346 km/h)
Service Ceiling:	20,000 ft (6,100 m)
Range:	700 miles (1,125 km)

THIS AIRCRAFT IS ON LOAN FROM THE NATIONAL MUSEUM OF THE USAF

Based on the Beech Model 18 commercial light transport, the C-45 was first ordered by the Army Air Corps in 1940. Ultimately both Army and Navy would use it in a variety of configurations. Passenger seating varied from six to eight in the various models.

U.S. Navy BuNo 51291 was built as an SNB-2 (later redesignated UC-45) and delivered on October 6, 1943. It served at a number of Naval Air Stations including NAS Patuxent River, Maryland, and NAS El Toro, California. It ended its Navy career at the Naval Weapons Lab at NAS Dahlgren, Maryland in June 1966 with over 12,000 hours in its logbook. The aircraft was delivered by truck to the museum in September 1988 and placed on display after restoration in April 1992. It is painted as a USAF C-45J, and given the S/N 42-51291.

DOUGLAS C-53D
SKYTROOPER

SPECIFICATIONS:

Crew:		3 plus up to 27 Troops, 18-24 litters, one or two gliders.
Dimensions:		
	Span:	95 ft 6 in. (29.1 m)
	Length:	63 ft 9 in. (19.4 m)
	Height:	17 ft 0 in. (5.2 m)
	Weight: Empty:	18,200 lbs. (8,254 kg)
	Gross:	26,000 (11,790 kg)
Performance:	Max. Speed:	230 mph (370 km/h)
	Ceiling:	24,000 ft. (7,315 m)
Power Plants:		Two Pratt & Whitney R-1830 engines
	Takeoff Power:	1,200 hp (895 kW)

THIS AIRCRAFT IS ON LOAN FROM THE NATIONAL MUSEUM OF THE USAF

Based upon the Douglas DC-3 airliner, the C-53 was one of several models made on the commercial production lines for the Army Air Forces during the early years of the war. Externally similar to the C-47, but without a reinforced floor or the double doors for loading cargo, the aircraft was designed to carry paratroops and tow gliders. They would also see service, however, transporting wounded, carrying cargo and towing gliders.

USAAF S/N 42-68835 is one of 150 C-53Ds built by Douglas Aircraft at Santa Monica, California (Factory S/N 11762), and delivered to the USAAF on July 12, 1943. It was assigned to the 72nd Troop Carrier Squadron, 434th Troop Carrier Group, while undergoing training with the 101st Airborne Division before departing for overseas in September 1943. Upon arrival in England, the Group was assigned to the 9th Troop Carrier Command, 9th Air Force; and the aircraft was assigned to Group Headquarters, but continued to be maintained by the 72nd TCS, whose markings it carried throughout the war. At dawn on D-Day, June 6, 1944, the 434th Group took the first 100 gliders into Normandy with the 101st Airborne. A total of three glider missions were flown in the first two days of the invasion. The Group would participate in the subsequent airborne operations in Holland, at Bastogne during the Battle of the Bulge, and finally in the final airborne operation over the Rhine River. It is known that our aircraft did participate in glider drops during the "Market Garden" operation in Holland.

The markings on the aircraft are based upon a photograph taken over France in January 1945, and indicate that the aircraft participated in three glider operations up to that time, as well as numerous medical evacuation and cargo missions. After the war the aircraft returned to the U.S. and was leased by American Airlines under Civilian Registration Number N19924. It would later be used by various government agencies before being sold to civilians. Ultimately it was seized by the Drug Enforcement Agency and offered to the USAF museum program. It was flown to the museum in June 1987, and restored to its original military configuration by the museum volunteers.

DOUGLAS C-54D *SKYMASTER*

SPECIFICATIONS:

CREW:		Five, with accommodations for 50 troops
DIMENSIONS:	Wing Span:	117 ft., 6 in. (35.8 m)
	Length:	93 ft., 10 in. (28.9 m)
	Height:	27 ft., 6 in. (8.34 m)
	Weight: Empty,	62,000 lbs. (28,118 kg)
	Max. Gross,	84,000 lbs. (38,095 kg)
PERFORMANCE:	Max. Speed:	265 mph (426 km/h)
	Service Ceiling:	22,000 ft. (6,700 m)
	Range:	3,900 mi. (6,275 km)
POWERPLANTS:		Four 1,350 hp (1,000 kW) Pratt & Whitney R-2000-11 engines

OWNED BY THE AEROSPACE MUSEUM OF CALIFORNIA, DONATED BY AERO UNION

The Douglas DC-4 was intended for the airlines; however with the onset of WWII in 1941 the US Army commandeered its production for use as a troop transport and cargo aircraft. To meet the demand Douglas constructed a new factory in Illinois just to build it. C-54s were operated extensively in both the Atlantic and Pacific Theaters during WWII by both the US Army Air Forces and the US Navy. In total C-54s made over 79,642 ocean crossings during the war with the loss of only three aircraft, two in the Atlantic, one in the Pacific.

The Museum's aircraft is the tenth of 380 C-54Ds, all of which were built at Douglas's purpose built Orchard Place factory (now O'Hare International Airport) near Chicago, Illinois. Their first C-54 aircraft took off on July 30, 1943, a year after construction was started on the factory. Our C-54-1-DC, s/n 10554, was built with USAAF Tail No. 42-72449, however on February 5, 1945 it was one of 94 new aircraft immediately transferred to the US Navy. There it was re-designated as their R5D-3 and assigned BuNo 50874. It served in a number of Naval Air Transport service squadrons during WWII and on into the 1950s, and is believed to have been on strength with VR6/VR8 when they set records hauling coal into Berlin during the Berlin Airlift. This likely explains the source of the fine, black dust that kept appearing when it was operated by Woods Hole during the 1960s. The records also show that BuNo 50874 was damaged in Germany, June 6, 1949, which was near the end of the airlift. Other assignments included VR-1, NAS (Naval Air Station) Patuxent River, Maryland, VR-8, Hickam AFB, Hawaii, VR-22, NAS Norfork, Virginia, VR-24 Port Lyautey, Morocco, and then in 1962 was redesignated as a C-54Q and transferred to Office of Naval Research, Boston, Massachusetts and operated by the Woods Hole Oceanographic Institute of Massachusetts in support of a new US Navy submarine detection system, wherein it often flew missions around the world.

In February 1970, the contract ended and the aircraft was flown to storage at Davis-Monthan AFB, Arizona. In September 1975, it was sold to Mercy Airlift, Ontario, California, who registered the aircraft as N27MA, but subsequently sold the aircraft to an aircraft leasing company. It was later apprehended delivering 9,820 pounds of marijuana to South Carolina from South America and was confiscated by the Drug Enforcement Agency. A private individual purchased the aircraft from the Sheriff and later sold it to Aero Union, of Chico, California, an aerial fire-fighting company. Aero Union delivered it to the Museum in January 1993. Douglas built a total of 1,244 C-54/DC-4 aircraft and licensees built an additional 71. Only 81 post-war DC-4s were built by Douglas as the demands from the airlines were satisfied with war surplus C-54s reconfigured for airline service. Our aircraft has been repainted as it would have been when first built, a C-54D with its original USAAF Tail Number, 42-72449.

AMC C-54Q at Woods Hole Oceanographic Inst.

FAIRCHILD C-119G
FLYING BOXCAR

SPECIFICATIONS:

Power Plants: Two 3,500 hp (2,610 kW) Wright R-3350-85 Turbo-Compound radial engines.

Dimensions:

Span:	109 ft 3 in (33.3 m)
Length:	86 ft 6 in (26.4 m)
Height:	26 ft 6 in (8.1 m)
Weight: Empty -	39,800 lbs (18,050 kg)
Maximum Gross -	74,000 lbs (33,560 kg)

Performance:

Maximum Speed:	281 mph (452 km/h) at 18,000 ft (5,500 m)
Service Ceiling:	23,900 ft (7,300 m)
Range:	1,770 miles (2,850 km)

THIS AIRCRAFT IS ON LOAN FROM THE NATIONAL MUSEUM OF THE USAF

The Fairchild C-119 was a larger and more powerful version of the Fairchild C-82 "Packet". It was designed to air-drop paratroops and large cargo. It features rear clamshell doors along with a monorail system for the delivery of items throughout the cargo compartment. Pratt & Whitney R-4360 engines powered initial versions, while later versions use the Wright R-3350-85 Turbo-compound engine, with gross weight increased to 85,000 lbs. A total of 1,185 C-119s were built, with the most produced version being the C-119G. C-119s served principally with Troop Carrier Command Wings, seeing service in Korea with the 314th Air Division. Several aircraft were modified in 1960 to use "snatch" techniques for mid-air recovery of space capsules during their descent from orbit. During the Vietnam War, some C-119s were converted to "gun-ships" (AC-119), and equipped with two 20 mm rotary barrel cannons in gun pods.

RCAF S/N 22114 is a C-119G built by Fairchild Aircraft at Hagerstown, Maryland and delivered to the Royal Canadian Air Force Air Transport Command on March 18, 1953. It served with various units including No. 436 Squadron at Downsview, and later Uplands, Ontario. It was flown to the RCAF Storage Area at Saskatoon, Saskatchewan on June 28, 1965; and sold to a private firm in the United States on February 1, 1967. The aircraft was flown to the museum from Greybull, Wyoming on October 24, 1988 after service as a fire bomber. It is currently painted in USAF markings.

LOCKHEED EC-121D
WARNING STAR

SPECIFICATIONS:

Crew:	22, including radar operators.
Power Plants:	Four 3,250 hp (2,424 kW) Wright R-3350-35 turbo-compound engines.
Dimensions:	
Span:	126 ft 2 in (38.5 m)
Length:	116 ft 2 in (35.4 m)
Height:	27 ft 0 in (8.2 m)
Weight: Empty -	80,611 lbs (36,560 kg)
Maximum Gross -	143,600 lbs (65,125 kg)
Performance:	
Speed:	321 mph (517 km/h) at 20,000 ft (6,100 m)
Service Ceiling:	20,600 ft (6,279 m)
Range:	4,600 miles (7,400 km)

THIS AIRCRAFT IS ON LOAN FROM THE NATIONAL MUSEUM OF THE USAF

Built by Lockheed Aircraft, it was derived from the Lockheed L-1049 "*Super Constellation*" commercial airliner for use as an airborne picket plane carrying special electronic gear. First developed by the US Navy, a similar variant was produced for USAF early warning airborne operations. The 552nd AEW & Control Wing began operations with the *Warning Star* in October 1953. Patrols off the U.S. West Coast were operated from McClellan AFB, California. During the Vietnam War, aircraft from the 552nd operated from airfields in South Vietnam providing early warning and control for aircraft flying missions over North Vietnam during Project "*College Eye*".

This aircraft is a Navy WV-2, BuNo 141309 (redesignated EC-121K in 1962 under the new Tri-Service Designation System), built by Lockheed Aircraft in Burbank, California and delivered to the Navy in August 1956. It served with VW-13, VW-15, and VW-2 at NAS Patuxent River, Maryland, and in November 1961 it was sent to the Pacific Missile Range, NAS Point Mugu, California. It was retired to Davis-Monthan AFB, Arizona in March 1978, and was flown to the museum in April 1983. The museum gave the "*Warning Star*" USAF S/N 53-552 in honor of the 552nd Airborne Early Warning and Control Wing, which was stationed at McClellan from 1953 to 1977 and flew EC-121D versions of the aircraft.

CONVAIR VC-131D
SAMARITAN

SPECIFICATIONS:

Crew:	**Three to four**
Power Plants:	**Two 2,500 hp (1,865 kW) Pratt-Whitney R-2800-99W radial engines**
Dimensions:	
Span:	**105 ft 4 in (32.1 m)**
Length:	**79 ft 2 in (24.1 m)**
Height:	**28 ft 2 in (8.6 m)**
Weight: Empty-	**29,248 lbs (13,264 kg)**
Maximum Gross-	**47,000 lbs (21,315 kg)**
Performance:	
Maximum Speed:	**293 mph (472 km/h)**
Cruise Speed:	**254 mph (410 km/h)**
Service Ceiling:	**24,500 ft (7,470 m)**
Range:	**1600-1900 miles (2,575-3,575 km)**

THIS AIRCRAFT IS ON LOAN FROM THE NATIONAL MUSEUM OF THE USAF

Based upon the Convair Model 440 commercial airliner, VC-131D aircraft were acquired for transporting government officials and dignitaries. With improved soundproofing over earlier Model 340 aircraft, they could comfortably seat up to 44 passengers. These aircraft were assigned to Headquarters units of various military commands throughout the world.

During its career, this aircraft served as transportation for a variety of dignitaries including Secretary of State Henry Kissinger, the Shah of Iran, prior to being allocated to California Air National Guard where it served as *"California One"*, the official aircraft for the Governor of California, and was used by Governors Brown and Deukmajian.

USAF S/N 54-2822 is a VC-131-CO, one of 16 built by Consolidated Vultee Aircraft (CONVAIR) in San Diego, California. It was delivered to the Air Force on March 15, 1955. It was first assigned to the 4500th Support Squadron (TAC), Langley AFB, Virginia. In December 1957 it moved to the 7100st Support Wing (USAFE), Wiesbaden AB, Germany; returning to the 4500th Support Squadron at Langley AFB, Virginia in February 1958. It was assigned to the 7415th Support Group (USAFE), Orly Field, Paris, France in September, 1958; then the 317th Air Base Group (USAFE), Evreux/Fauville AB, France in October, 1958; the 513th Troop Carrier Wing (USAFE), Orly Field, France in April, 1966; the 7101st Air Base Wing (USAFE), Chievres, Belgium and Echterdingen Army Field, Germany in October, 1967; to the Military Assistance Group (USAFE), Teheran, Iran in July, 1973; and the 144th Fighter Interceptor Wing (ANG), Fresno, California in May, 1978. While with the 144th the aircraft was known as "California One", and it was based for much of the time at McClellan AFB, Sacramento. The aircraft was presented to the museum after its final flight on June 27, 1989.

BOEING 727-225F

727-225 s/n 21292 as FedEx N466FE, Takeoff from Ottawa, Canada in 2005. Photo by S.A. Kelly

SPECIFICATIONS:

CREW:		Three (Pilot, Co-pilot and Flight Engineer)
DIMENSIONS:	Wing Span:	108 ft. (32.9 m)
	Length:	153 ft., 2 in. (46.7 m)
	Tail Height:	34 ft., 11 in. (10.6 m)
	Empty Weight:	98,040 lbs. (44,463 kg)
	Max. Takeoff Weight:	197,000 lbs. (89,342 kg)
PERFOREMANCE:	Cruising Speed:	570 mph (917 km/h)
	Service Ceiling:	42,000 ft. (12,800 m)
	Range:	2,150 mi. (3,460 km)
POWER PLANTS:		Three Pratt & Whitney JT8D-15 engines
	Takeoff Thrust, each:	15,500 lbs. (68.9 kN)

AIRCRAFT IS ON LOAN FROM SACRAMENTO CITY COLLEGE FOLLOWING DONATION TO THEM BY FEDEX

The Boeing 727 was announced December 5, 1960 as the first commercial tri-jet and was designed to service smaller airports with shorter runways than those used by earlier jets. It first flew in February 1963, introducing completely powered flight controls, triple-slotted flaps and an onboard auxiliary power unit (APU).

Boeing hoped to build 250 of the airplanes; however, it proved so popular with the airlines and passengers (especially after the longer 727-200 Advanced model was introduced in 1967) that a total of 1,832 had been produced when production ended in August 1984. The aircraft was available in passenger, convertible passenger-cargo, and an all-cargo variant. Many passenger 727 airplanes were later converted to freighters, which is the case with the museum's example. The military also used the 727 for personnel transport, designating them as C-22s.

The Museum's aircraft is the 1240th Boeing 727, s/n 21292. The aircraft was delivered to Eastern Airlines on December 21, 1976, were it operated in passenger service as N8874Z until June 1989 when it was leased to Avianca Airlines, Colombia's flag carrier. It was returned to Eastern Airlines for retirement in December 1990.

Federal Express (*FedEx*) purchased the aircraft in 1992 and converted it to a Boeing 727-225F freighter. *FedEx* began operating the aircraft in July 1992 in their small package and cargo service as N466FE. The aircraft remained in service with *FedEx* until it was retired and donated to the Sacramento City College Aeronautics Department on February 15, 2013, and in partnership with the Aerospace Museum of California, has found a very good home here at the museum. During its 37 year flying career s/n 21292 accumulated a total of 55,481 flying hours and 39,722 landings.

The aircraft is named *"Gideon"* in honor of a child of a *FedEx* flight crew member

727-225 s/n 21292 as Eastern N8874Z, Oct 1990,
Washington, D.C. Photo by George W Hamlin

TAYLORCRAFT L-2M *GRASSHOPPER*

SPECIFICATIONS:

Crew:	Two
Power Plant:	One 65 hp (48.5 kW) Continental O-170-3 four cylinder air-cooled engine
Dimensions:	
Span:	35 ft 5 in (10.8 m)
Length:	22 ft 9 in (6.9 m)
Height:	8 ft 0 in (2.4 m)
Weight: Empty -	875 lbs (397 kg)
Maximum Gross -	1,300 lbs (590 kg)
Performance:	
Maximum Speed:	88 mph 142 km/h)
Service Ceiling:	10,050 ft (3,060 m)
Range:	230 miles (370 km)

THIS AIRCRAFT IS ON LOAN FROM THE NATIONAL MUSEUM OF THE USAF

Originally known as the YO-57, the Taylorcraft L-2 came from the commercial Taylorcraft Model D, and was one of a series of light aircraft used in the observation and liaison mission during World War II. The L-2 featured a high-wing, tandem seats, and dual controls, and was first tested by the Army in 1941 along with the Aeronca YO-58, and the Piper YO-59. All three types were ordered, and all were known as "*Grasshoppers*". The L-2M was the final version of the L-2, and featured a fully cowled engine, and the fitting of wing spoilers. All of the aircraft were unarmed.

USAAF S/N 43-26433 was one of 900 L-2M aircraft built by Taylorcraft Aviation Corp., in Alliance, Ohio. It was delivered to the USAAF on December 9, 1943 and assigned to the Civil Air Patrol in Little Rock, Arkansas on December 12, 1943. It was dropped from the USAAF inventory in July 1945 and entered civilian use until flown to the museum on September 11, 1985.

GRUMMAN TS-2A *TRACKER*

SPECIFICATIONS:

Crew:	Three
Powerplants:	Two Wright R-1820-82WA Cyclones each rated at 1,525 hp (1,137 kW)
Dimensions:	
Wing span –	72 ft 7 in (22.1 m)
Wings folded, span –	27 ft 4 in (8.3 m)
Length –	43 ft 6 in (13.3 m)
Height –	16 ft 7 in (5.1 m)
Weight, Empty: –	18.750 lbs (8,500 kg)
Maximum Gross–	29,150 lbs (13,220 kg)
Performance:	
Speed, maximum at Sea level –	265 mph (425 km/h)
Cruise speed –	207 mph (333 km/h)
Ceiling:	21,000 ft (6,400 m)
Range:	1,000 miles (1,609 km)

OWNED BY AEROSPACE MUSEUM OF CALIFORNIA

One of the most successful anti-submarine warfare (ASW) aircraft yet conceived, the Tracker first flew in December 1952, and entered service with the U.S. Navy in 1954. It was continuously updated for ASW service, though many of the earlier machines found work as utility and training aircraft.

Our aircraft, TS-2A BuNo 133251, was one of the early model S-2s used in non-tactical roles and for training multi-engine flight crews until replaced by the Beech T-44A in 1980.

Upon retirement, most of the S-2s went into storage, from where some would see service with foreign air forces, while others were transferred to various Forestry Services of the various states and converted to fire fighting duties.

The Naval service of BuNo 133251 is not known, but it was operated by the California Division of Forestry and flew as a fire bomber many years; it carries the CDF markings including the number "78" on the rudder. Recently it was retired and sold to a private owner, Tim Morrow of Atlanta, Georgia, along with several others. He in turn donated the aircraft to the Aerospace Museum of California.

GRUMMAN HU-16B/E *ALBATROSS*

SPECIFICATIONS:

Crew: Two pilots, navigator, radio operator and two medical attendants.
Powerplants: Two 1,425 hp (1,060 kW) Wright R-1820-76 radial engines.
Dimensions:

Span:	96 ft 8 in (29.5 m)
Length:	61 ft 3 in (18.7 m)
Height:	25 ft 10 in (7.9 m)
Weight: Empty -	22,883 lbs (10,375 kg)
Maximum Gross -	32,000 lbs (14,500 kg)

Performance:

Max. Speed:	236 mph (380 km/h) at 18,800 ft (5,500 m)
Service Ceiling:	25,000 ft (7,600 m)
Range:	3,220 miles (5,180 km)

THIS AIRCRAFT IS ON LOAN FROM THE NATIONAL MUSEUM OF THE USAF

The HU-16 is the largest twin engine amphibian built by Grumman Aircraft. The "*Albatross*" was able to operate from land, water, and snow and ice when fitted with skis. The USAF ordered 297 aircraft for use in the air-sea rescue role. The prototype made its first flight on October 24, 1947. In the Korean and Vietnam Wars it was credited with hundreds of rescues, and besides the USAF, it also saw service with the U.S. Coast Guard, U.S. Navy, and 22 foreign countries. The original designation for the "*Albatross*" was SA-16. The -B model was the result of a 16-1/2 foot increase in the wing span. In 1962 the designation was changed to HU-16, and in Coast Guard service the HU-16B was known as the HU-16E.

USAF S/N 51-7209 is a HU-16B, one of 464 built by Grumman Aircraft in Bethpage, New York. It was delivered to the USAF on July 16, 1953 and assigned to the 1707th Training Squadron (MATS), Palm Beach, Florida. In May 1959 it was deployed to Brookley AFB, Alabama; and in March 1960 it was sent for storage at Davis-Monthan AFB, Arizona. In April 1961 it was transferred to the U.S. Coast Guard and assigned to CG Station Port Angeles, Washington. Its last two assignments were CG Station Corpus Christi, Texas in August 1975, and CG Station Traverse City, Michigan in March 1978. In October 1978 it was flown to Luke AFB, Arizona for display, and on March 28, 1988 it was carried by a C-5 to McClellan AFB for restoration and display in the museum. It was restored by the CG Station McClellan, and bears appropriate Coast Guard markings.

DASSAULT HU-25A
GUARDIAN

SPECIFICATIONS:		
CREW:		2 Pilots and 3 Systems Operators
DIMENSIONS:	Length:	56 ft 3 in (17.1 m)
	Wingspan:	53 ft 6 in (16.3 m)
	Height:	17 ft 7 in (5.4 m)
	Empty Weight:	19,700 lbs (8,932 kg)
	Max takeoff weight:	33,510 lbs (16,104 kg)
PERFORMANCE:	Max speed:	437 mph (703 km/h) at 20,000 ft
	Cruise speed:	404 mph (650 km/h) at 40,000 ft
	Range:	2,045 miles (3,290 km)
	Service Ceiling:	42,000 ft (12,800 m)
MISSION ENDURANCE:		5+ hours with 1,534 gals (6,757 liters)
POWERPLANTS:		2 Garrett ATF3-6-4C Turbofan engines
	Takeoff Thrust, each:	5,440 lbs (24.2 kN)

OWNED BY THE AEROSPACE MUSEUM OF CALIFORNIA

The HU-25 *Guardian* is a jet powered multi-mission maritime patrol and surveillance version of the Dassault Falcon 20G, a French business jet that first flew in 1963. A total of 41 HU-25A aircraft were assembled in Little Rock, Arkansas and delivered to the US Coast Guard between April 1981 and December 1983. The aircraft performs search and rescue (SAR), drug and migrant interdiction, fisheries and law enforcement, marine environmental protection, defense readiness and essential mission logistics. All subsequent versions were converted from the original "A" models, including seven as HU-25Bs to operate the AIREYE surveillance system, designed to locate and track oil spills and other pollution at sea. HU-25 use by the US Coast Guard will end in 2014.

USCG #2118 was the 18th HU-25A accepted by the US Coast Guard and in March 1985 was the first modified to the HU-25B configuration. #2118 spent most of its career rotating between Air Stations at Miami, Florida; Cape Cod, Massachusetts; Corpus Christie, Texas; and the Aviation Training Center (ATC) in Mobile, Alabama.

During OPERATION DESERT STORM in February 1991 #2118 was one of two *Guardians* dispatched to the theatre as a result of Iraqi destroyed oil wells and oil pumping stations causing massive oil spills. As part of a US interagency oil spill assessment team they mapped over 40,000 square miles of coastline in 84 days of deployment.

Later in 1991 #2118 was operating out of Air Station Cape Cod and performed a number of missions associated with the "Perfect Storm" of October 1991, which was made into a movie of the same name. In October 2003 the AIREYE system was removed and #2118 reverted back to the HU-25A configuration. The aircraft was removed from active service in October 2010 and stored at Coast Guard Air Station Sacramento. It was declared as surplus property in October 2013, and the Museum acquired it through the Federal Surplus Property Program.

MAKANI M600 *ENERGY KITE*

SPECIFICATIONS:

CREW:		Internal and Remote Control
DIMENSIONS:	Wing Span:	83 ft., 4 in. (25.4 m)
	Wing Aspect Ratio:	20:1
	Wing Area:	344.4 sq. ft. (32 sq m)
	Length:	33 ft., 5 in. (10.2 m)
	Height:	18 ft., 0 in. (5.5 m)
	Weight:	4,096 lbs. (1,854 kg)
PERFORMANCE:	Wind Speed for 600 kW:	18.0 mph (8 m/s)
	Minimum Wind Speed:	9.0 mph (4 m/s)
	Maximum Power Wind Speed, 1,000 kW:	25.7 mph (11.5 m/s)
	Maximum Operating Wind Speed, 1,000 kW:	55.9 mph (25 m/s)
	Maximum Structural Wind Speed:	145.4 mph (65 m/s)
	Optimum Loop Radius:	475 ft (145 m)
	Service Ceiling:	460 to 1,017 ft. (140 to 310 m)
POWERPLANTS:		
	Rotor/Propeller diameters:	7 ft., 6.5 in. (2.3 m)
	Eight 100 hp (75 kW) Permanent Magnetic Core Motor/Generators	
	Teather Power Transmission	1,700 vDC

OWNED BY THE AEROSPACE MUSEUM OF CALIFORNIA

M600 in Launch/Recovery attitude during 2019 tests in North Sea

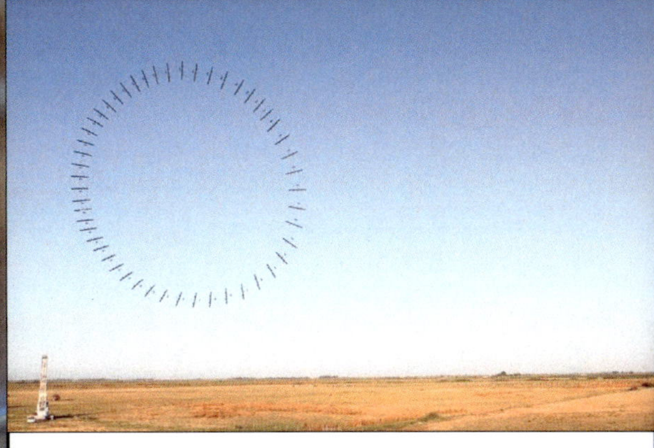

M600 in Crosswind Flight, composite photo by Makani & Thomas van Alsenoy

The Makani M600 was an experimental program at "X", Alphabet's "moonshot factory", formerly Google [X], and a pioneer in the emerging field of airborne wind energy. The program was intended to drastically reduce the cost and environmental impact of renewable energy by operating in windy offshore locations. To this end the 13 year project was successful in demonstrating the M600 in both California and Hawaii. In 2020 Google announced they were terminating the project and released a vast body of knowledge and industrial know-how in open access, including a non-assertion pledge on 127 patents resulting from the project. The termination decision was made "Despite strong technical progress, the road to commercialization is longer and riskier than hoped."

The nominally 26 meter wingspan M600 was the cumulation of several smaller development kites and was designed in 2014. It is largely built of carbon fiber composites and utilizes a wing airfoil tailored for its unique flight path, speeds and dynamic loading.

To begin a flight the kite is perched on a base station which turns to position the kite downwind. The kites rotors are initially electrically driven by the eight motor/generators to rise into a vertical hover, much like a helicopter. The 500 meter electricity conducting tether/cable is then played out, allowing the M600 to rise into the wind. Once in horizontal flight the wind-driven propellers transition to the generator mode, wherein the power of the wind is generating electricity, with rated capacity being 600 kW in an 18 mph wind. To maximize power generation the kite flies in vertical loops across the wind, effectively "tacking," much as a sailboat does to maximize speed. To end the flight the kite is reeled in and transitions back into a controlled hover and sets down upon its base station. During flight the M600 is controlled by onboard computers and software utilizing GPS and other sensors to steer the kite.

A total of seven M600s were built; however only the AMC displayed example has been preserved, donated by Alphabet, Inc.

Appendix A
Aerospace Museum of California Aircraft Collection

Aircraft	Type	Status	Owned By	Serial or Tail No.
Grumman G-165A, *Ag-Cat*	Ag Sprayer	Storage	AMC-Donated by Chuck Proctor	
Douglas A-1E	Attack Bomber	Display-AirPark	On Loan from National Museum of USAF	BUNO 132463
Douglas A-4C	Attack Bomber	Display-AirPark	On Loan from National Mus of Naval Aviation	BUNO 148503
Fairchild A-10A	Attack Bomber	Display-AirPark	On Loan from National Museum of USAF	76-540
Vought A-7D	Attack Bomber	Display-AirPark	On Loan from National Museum of USAF	70-0998
CEI BQM-167 *Skeeter*	Drone-Aerial Target	Display-Pavilion	On Loan from CEI Corp, Sacramento, CA	NA
Northrop MQM-36A *Shelduck*	Drone-Aerial Target	Storage	AMC-Donated by Jeffery Travis Parker	MQ11881
Lockheed F-80B	Fighter/Bomber	Display-AirPark	On Loan from National Museum of USAF	45-8704
Republic F-84F	Fighter/Bomber	Display-AirPark	On Loan from National Museum of USAF	51-1772
North American F-86F	Fighter/Bomber	Display-AirPark	On Loan from National Museum of USAF	51-13082
North American F-100D	Fighter/Bomber	Display-AirPark	On Loan from National Museum of USAF	56-3288
Republic F-105D	Fighter/Bomber	Display-AirPark	On Loan from National Museum of USAF	62-4301
McDonnell F-4C	Fighter/Bomber	Display-AirPark	On Loan from National Museum of USAF	64-0706
General Dynamics FB-111A	Fighter/Bomber	Display-AirPark	On Loan from National Museum of USAF	67-0159
North American F-86L	Fighter/Interceptor	Display-AirPark	On Loan from National Museum of USAF	51-2968
McDonnell F-101B	Fighter/Interceptor	Display-AirPark	On Loan from National Museum of USAF	57-427
Convair F-102A	Fighter/Interceptor	Display-AirPark	On Loan from National Museum of USAF	56-1140
Lockheed F-104B	Fighter/Interceptor	Display-AirPark	On Loan from National Museum of USAF	57-1303
Convair F-106A	Fighter/Interceptor	Display-AirPark	On Loan from National Museum of USAF	59-00010
Grumman F-14D	Fighter/Interceptor	Display-AirPark	On Loan from Nat Mus of Naval Aviation	BUNO 163897
Mikoyan-Gurevich Mig-17PF	Fighter/Interceptor	Display-AirPark	On Loan from National Museum of USAF	1186, 4721?
Mikoyan-Gurevich Mig-21F	Fighter/Interceptor	Display-AirPark	On Loan from National Museum of USAF	0201?
Piasecki CH-21C *Workhorse*	Helicopter	Display-AirPark	Aerospace Museum of California	51-15886
QH-50D *DASH*	Helicopter	Display-Pavilion	Aerospace Museum of California	SN DS-1660
Sikorsky CH-3E	Helicopter	Display-AirPark	On Loan from National Museum of USAF	65-5690
Aerojet *Aerobee 350*	Sounding Rocket	Display-Pavilion	On Loan from National Air & Space Museum	SN NACA-014
Aerojet Delta II Second Stage	Space Rocket	Display-Pavilion	AMC-Donated by Aerojet-Rocketdyne	NA
Raven RX-7 Hot Air Balloon	Sport-Balloon	Display-Pavilion	AMC-Donated by Byron Stevenson	RX7-331/N4099V
Pacific *Klassic* Hang Glider	Sport-Hang Glider	Storage	AMC-Donated by Shawn Mathews	NA
Pober *Pixie*	Sport-Homebuilt	Storage	On Loan from Robert Gilbert Family	N7035M
Rutan Model 54 *Quickie*	Sport-Homebuilt	Display-Pavilion	AMC-Donated, John Macomas & Bill Mauser	
Robinson Model 5 Sail-Plane	Sport-Homebuilt	Storage	AMC-Donated by William Rush	
Bellmore *Flightstar II SL*	Sport-Light Sport	Storage	AMC-Donated by Jerry Bellmore	N9080V
Pitts S-1C *Special*	Sport-Racer, Bi-Plane	Display-Pavilion	AMC-Donated by John Adler, Tom Strueber, & Deanes Rowedder	N382SJ

Appendix A

Aerospace Museum of California Aircraft Collection

Aircraft	Type	Status	Owned By	Serial or Tail No.
North American T-6G	Trainer-Advanced	Display-AirPark	On Loan from National Museum of USAF	51-15124
North American T-28B	Trainer-Advanced	Display-AirPark	On Loan from National Museum of USAF	BUNO 138327
Lockheed T-33A	Trainer-Advanced	Display-AirPark	On Loan from National Museum of USAF	53-5205
Hunting/BAC *Jet Provost* TMk3A	Trainer-Advanced	Display-AirPark	On Loan from Jon Todd & Ken McDermott	XN472/N69RT
Fairchild PT-19B	Trainer-Primary	Display-Pavilion	AMC-Restored, Saved from Salvage	42-83234
Beech UC-45J	Transport/Utility	Display-AirPark	On Loan from National Museum of USAF	BUNO 51291
Douglas C-53D	Transport/Cargo	Display-AirPark	On Loan from National Museum of USAF	42-68835
Douglas C-54D	Transport/Cargo	Display-AirPark	Aerospace Museum of California	42-72499
Fairchild C-119F	Transport/Cargo	Display-AirPark	On Loan from National Museum of USAF	SN 22114
Grumman TS-2A	Transport/Radar	Display-AirPark	AMC-Donated by Tim Morrow, Atlanta GA	SN 222
Lockheed EC-121K	Transport/Radar	Display-AirPark	On Loan from National Museum of USAF	BUNO 141309
Grumman HU-16E	Transport/Rescue	Display-AirPark	On Loan from National Museum of USAF	USCG 7209/51-7209
Dassault HU-25A	Transport/Rescue	Display-AirPark	AMC-Acquired as Surplus Federal Property	USCG 2118
Taylorcraft L-2M	Transport/Spotter	Display-Pavilion	On Loan from National Museum of USAF	N53792 & 45-745
North American T-39A	Transport/Trainer	Display-AirPark	On Loan from National Museum of USAF	61-0660
Convair VC-131D	Transport/VIP	Display-AirPark	On Loan from National Museum of USAF	54-2822
Boeing 727-225F	Transport/Freighter	Display-AirPark	On Loan from Sacramento City College	SN 21292/N466FE

NOTE: Model designations and serial numbers as recorded on museum records. Aircraft may be displayed otherwise. Approximately 50 aircraft and aerospace vehicles in the collection as of January 2023.

Appendix B

Aircraft Designations

Aircraft names and designations can sometimes be confusing; the reason for this is that every manufacturer and operating organization tends to construct a system that meets their purposes. There is no single set of rules on how to proceed.

Military designations are most prevalent at the museum as ex-military aircraft form the base of the collection. With that there are some general rules that will aide in understanding the time period and mission of a particular aircraft.

The USAF carried on with the old US Army designations when they became a separate force in 1947. That system uses a letter to describe the type of aircraft, such as A-Attack, B-Bomber, C-Cargo/Transport, F-Fighter (P-Pursuits in Army terminology), H-Helicopter and T-Trainer. A sequence number, such as F-100, F-101, and F-102, then identified individual aircraft developed within these categories. Specific mission capabilities designed in to the aircraft would result in a prefix letter, E- Electronics, R-Reconnaissance, U-Utility, P-Primary, A-Attack, V-VIP. This results in designations such as AT-33 for an armed T-33 trainer, and for the radar picket EC-121 *Warning Star* version of the C-121 transport.

Suffixes are added to the sequence number to identify major modifications or new models within a type. The F-104B is a two-seat trainer version of the F-104A Interceptor and the F-105D is an improved version of the earlier type having a more powerful engine and upgraded weapons systems. Two letters designating the manufacturer then follow, and some aircraft also received a block number related to specific procurement or equipment configurations.

Navy aircraft used an entirely different scheme. It was based on a type letter, A-Attack, B-Bomber, C-Cargo, F-Fighter, P-Patrol, which was then followed by a design sequence number relative to the aircrafts manufacturer, followed by a third letter designating the manufacturer. For example, the A4D was the 4th attack type built by Douglas Aircraft Co., and the AD-5, which was the first attack type from Douglas. The dash 5 indicates that this model was the fifth major model of the type. Other examples are the F4U-1D *Corsair* fighter designed and built by Chance Vought during WWII. This same aircraft was also built by Goodyear Corporation and identified as the FG-1D, and by Brewster, where it was designated the F3A-1.

In the late 1950s and early 1960s the USAF was purchasing models of the Navy's F4H *Phantom II*, which they designated as the F-110A, and the Navy the Air Force's aircraft which also carried dual designations. This confused Congress and resulted in an entirely new DOD wide designation system. It retained much of the old Air Force system, but the sequence numbers were restarted, often adopting the corresponding number from the Navy. This resulted in the Navy's *Phantom II* being designated as F-4C for the Air Force and F-4B for the Navy. The museum's Navy F-14D *Tomcat* is an example of this new scheme, as are the Air Forces F-15 and F-16.

Manufacturers like to have their name in the designation of their airplanes. Examples are the Pitts S-1C biplane and the Mikoyan-Gurevich MiG-21 supersonic jet interceptor.

The British typically name their aircraft, such as the *Jet Provost*, and then add mission specific designations such as T Mk 3A, signifying the aircraft's mission is "Training" and the "Mark 3A" is the configuration standard.

Made in the USA
Middletown, DE
22 March 2024